VOLUME 9

McDONNELL DOUGLAS
F-15 EAGLE

BY DENNIS R. JENKINS

specialtypress
PUBLISHERS AND WHOLESALERS

Published by
Specialty Press Publishers and Wholesalers
11481 Kost Dam Road
North Branch, MN 55056
United States of America
(612) 583-3239

Distributed in the UK and Europe by
Airlife Publishing Ltd.
101 Longden Road
Shrewsbury
SY3 9EB
England

ISBN 0-933424-72-8

Designed by Greg Compton

Printed in the United States of America

TABLE OF CONTENTS

THE MCDONNELL DOUGLAS F-15 EAGLE

PREFACE

Twenty-five years after its first flight, the McDonnell Douglas F-15 Eagle is still considered the world's most formidable air superiority fighter. Although conceived during the late 1960s and early 1970s, it has scored an impressive number of air-to-air kills in the late 1980s and 1990s, by most accounts approaching 100, with no known air-to-air losses. It has also, in its Strike Eagle variant, gained a considerable long-range air-to-ground interdiction capability that was well demonstrated in the Gulf War. The F-15 has been in constant production for over twenty years, with at least three more years worth already ordered. Well over 1,500 Eagles have been produced on two production lines: one in St. Louis, and one in Japan; and the F-15 is currently in service with the air forces of Israel, Japan, Saudi Arabia, and the United States.

But the F-15 is not the perfect fighter. Many knowledgeable people, including many of its pilots, complain that it is too large and heavy. A good point, although it has not hurt its maneuverability since in many flight regimes the Eagle can outmaneuver the smaller and less capable F-16. But the aircraft is undeniably large. Dimensionally it approximates the North American B-25 Mitchell from World War Two. In terms of maximum take-off weight, it is much closer to the Boeing B-17G Flying Fortress, and is almost four times heavier than the famed P-51 Mustang. And the F-15E can carry more payload than the Boeing B-29 Super Fortress.

The largest shortfall the F-15 exhibits is a less than ideal fuel-fraction (internal fuel weight as a percentage of take-off weight). This explains the fact that you seldom see an F-15 without at least one external fuel tank or conformal tanks. Luckily, the tanks are rated to the full maneuvering envelope (+9g) of the aircraft. And performance is available in abundance. The F-15 was the first USAF fighter with a combat thrust-to-weight ratio greater than 1:1, and the aircraft is capable of accelerating through Mach 1.0 in a vertical climb.

Many of the same problems that haunted other early turbofan equipped fighters (F-111, F-14, etc.) also plagued the F-15. The engines were unreliable, and tended to stall or stagnate at the most inopportune moments. Mostly these problems were cured by the addition of digital electronic engine controls, roughly akin to modern fuel injection on automobiles. It goes to show how expectations have changed, however, to realize that "unreliable" in this case meant that the engine stalled approximately once in every 100 flight hours. The first jet fighter, the Me 262, introduced into service only 30 years earlier, was lucky if its engines lasted 10 hours! Current F-15 statistics show a stall approximately every 1,000 hours, considered acceptable for a high performance engine. Regardless of the early engine problems, the F-15 has earned the distinction of being the safest (fewest accidents per flight hour) fighter in the history of the Air Force.

Most of the early F-15s (74-0116 shown here) have been transferred to Air National Guard units. However, this does not imply that the aircraft are not as capable as later models. The MSIP program has brought most F-15A/Bs up to basically the same standard as the F-15C/D, and the aircraft are still well within their airframe life expectancies. (Daniel Soulaine via the Mick Roth Collection)

WARBIRDTECH
S E R I E S

How long the F-15 continues in front-line service with the USAF depends largely on the fate of the Lockheed F-22 advanced tactical fighter designed to replace it. It has been over seven years since the YF-22 prototype first flew, and the first pre-production aircraft is still months away from flying.

The F-22 is almost twice as expensive as the $46 million F-15, and with the downfall of the Soviet Union, many question whether the expense is worth it. And new possibilities are on the horizon for the F-15. The ACTIVE project is demonstrating multi-directional thrust vectoring engines, further increasing the maneuverability of the Eagle. New weapons, both air-to-ground and air-to-air, have been added to the Eagle's arsenal, and new electronics are coming. Israel and Saudi Arabia are investing bil-

Fifteen years after production of the F-15 began, the F-15E "Mud Hen" arrived on the scene to show Saddam Hussein that air power could still decide the outcome of even the "mother of all Wars." Unlike previous F-15s, the Strike Eagle is optimized for air-to-ground combat, but it has given up little of its air-to-air capabilities along the way. The Weapons School at Nellis AFB operates several F-15Es, shown here with LANTIRN pods and a travel pod on the CFT. (J. E. Michaels via the Mick Roth Collection)

lions of dollars in the belief that the F-15 will reign supreme well into the next century. Time will tell, but don't bet against it.

I would like to thank Mick Roth; Stefaan Vanhastel; Tsahi Ben-Ami; Todd Enlund; Masahiro "Scotch" Koizumi; Dave Phillips, McAir; Chris M. Reed; Wesley B. Henry, Air Force Museum; C. E. 'Bud" Anderson; Col. Wendall "Wendy" Shawler; LtCol. Roger Smith, USAF; Cheryl Agin-Heathcock, Tony Landis and Don Gatlin, NASA/DFRC; Frederick Johnsen, AFFTC History Office; and Jay Miller.

DENNIS R. JENKINS
1997

The N-F-15B ACTIVE (Advanced Control Technology for Integrated Vehicles) is a major modification of the first TF-15A (71-0290). Currently flying at the NASA Dryden Flight Research Center, ACTIVE is demonstrating advanced thrust vectoring nozzles, and on 31 October 1996 performed the first known Mach 2 thrust vectoring maneuver. (NASA/Dryden)

ENERGY MANEUVERABILITY

The birth of a modern combat aircraft is not a single point in time. It begins with the government announcing a need, or a contractor believing it has developed something new. In most cases the first step is for the government to fund studies by several contractors to help validate a concept. These studies are evaluated, and if the results are promising, another study can be issued. Along the way, contracts for various specific research projects, such as developing a new weapon or radar for the aircraft, can be issued. At each step, the government takes the parts it likes of each result and folds them into the next phase. Eventually sufficient foundation exists for the government to issue a Request for Proposals (RFP) for the actual aircraft is desires. In theory, anybody can usually submit a proposal in response to an RFP. In reality, the competition is the same small group of aerospace giants since they are the only ones with the resources to respond to the RFP (the response may total many thousands of pages, involving thousands of hours of research). They are also the only ones with the resources to actually develop and build a complex modern aircraft and to meet the myriad of government rules and regulations.

The F-15 has its origins on 6 October 1965, when the Air Force issued Qualitative Operational Requirement 65-14F which defined what later became the F-X (Fighter-Experimental) project. On 8 December 1965 the aircraft industry was invited to study the requirement for an advanced tactical fighter that could replace the McDonnell F-4 Phantom II. Such an aircraft would need to be capable of establishing air superiority against all threats

This early illustration is one of the few released that show the proposed configuration at contract award. Noteworthy are the ventral fins, and the small vertical stabilizers. The nose is also significantly more pointed than the final aircraft. Armament is four AIM-82A short-range missiles and two AIM-7 medium-range Sparrows on the fuselage stations. The XAIM-82 project was cancelled before the F-15 first flew. (McDonnell Douglas)

F-X CONFIGURATION EVOLUTION

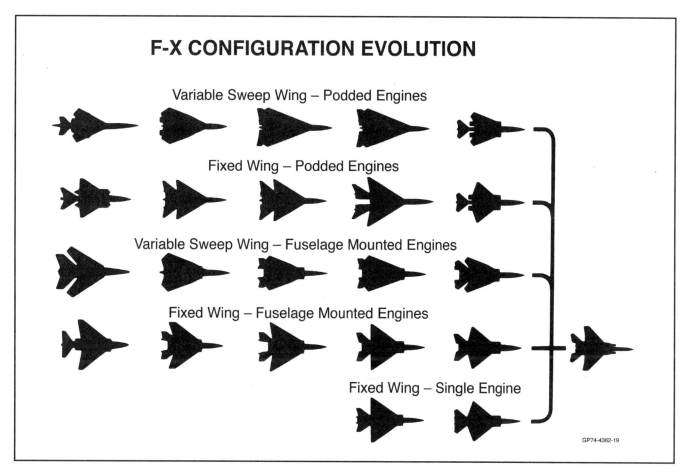

As part of the engineering studies during the F-X competition, McDonnell Douglas investigated numerous configurations for the F-15. Most of the designs were parametric variations on a theme, and over 1,000 configurations were ultimately studied. Interestingly, the F-15 shows a direct lineage to the F-4 (far left, 4th row from the top). Several of the designs look remarkably similar to proposals later submitted for the Advanced Tactical Fighter (ATF) that will eventually replace the F-15. (McDonnell Douglas)

projected for the post-1975 period, while also being able to perform a secondary air-to-ground mission. The Air Force envisioned this being a 60,000-pound variable-geometry wing Mach 2.5+ aircraft powered by a pair of advanced turbofan engines. Boeing, Grumman, Lockheed, McDonnell, and North American all began work on initial concept studies.

After looking over the results of these studies, the Air Force issued 60-day Concept Formulation Study contracts to Boeing, Lockheed, and North American in March 1966 to further refine the F-X. Grumman and McDonnell continued their studies using internal funds. However, the Air Force was not particularly impressed with any of the results, primarily because the aerodynamic configurations and engine technology were considered inadequate. Work proceeded at a slow pace from mid-1966 through 1967 while the Air Force pondered what to do next. The Air Force Systems Command sensed that the F-X requirements were "... badly spelled out ...", and was subsequently able to modify the requirements, thanks in a large part to the work of Maj. John R. Boyd.

A veteran pilot of the late-1950s, and author of an air combat manual used by the Fighter Weapons School, Boyd was well qualified to assess fighter aircraft. In 1962, while completing an engineering course at Georgia Tech, he studied the energy changes incurred by an aircraft during flight, and devised a method to measure aircraft maneuverability—the ability to change altitude, airspeed, and direction. Boyd continued his energy maneuverability studies at his next assignment at Eglin AFB, Florida, where he met mathematician Thomas Christie.

In May 1964 Boyd and Christie published a two-volume report on energy maneuverability, and

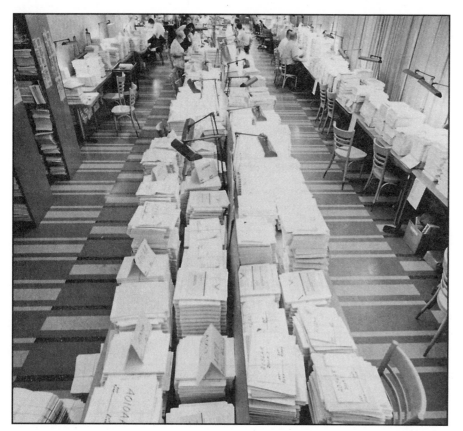

This is the amount of paper required to respond to the Air Force's Request for Proposal (RFP). A total of 2.5 million man-hours of effort had culminated in a 37,500 page proposal, and multiple copies had to be provided to the government. The McAir proposal, and subsequent development effort, was led by F-15 General Manager Donald Malvern. (McDonnell Douglas)

craft types, including the MiG-25 Foxbat (at the time thought to be the MiG-23), as well as several new versions of older aircraft. The Mach 2.8 performance of the Foxbat sufficiently alarmed Air Force officials that work on the F-X was assigned a higher priority, and on 11 August 1967, a second Concept Formulation Study RFP was issued. Fairchild-Republic, General Dynamics, Grumman, Lockheed, McDonnell Douglas, and North American submitted proposals, and on 1 December 1967 General Dynamics and McDonnell Douglas were contracted for the study. Most of the other contractors continued various related studies with their own internal funds.

although the theory did not represent anything new in terms of physics or aerodynamics, it formalized a method for developers to compare competing aircraft directly and to demonstrate the effects of design changes on aircraft performance. In October 1966, Boyd joined the Air Staff, and when asked to comment on the just completed F-X studies, he summarily rejected all of the designs as inappropriate to the task.

Several 3/8th scale F-15 models were dropped from the NASA/Dryden NB-52, using an adapter to attach them to the pylon originally developed for the X-15 program. One of the models continued in service with NASA for several years as the Spin Research Vehicle (SRV). The NB-52 shows all of its mission marks, ranging from the X-15, to the lifting bodies, and various other programs that have used the NB-52 to get airborne. (NASA/Dryden)

On 28 April 1967, the McDonnell Aircraft Company merged with the Douglas Aircraft Corporation, becoming the McDonnell Douglas Corporation, although each of the old companies continued to operate much as before.

In July 1967, the Russians held the famous Domodadovo air show where they introduced six new air-

By this time, through the efforts of Boyd and others, the projected

WARBIRD**TECH**
SERIES

weight of the F-X had been lowered from 60,000+ pounds to slightly under 40,000 pounds, and the required top speed reduced to Mach 2.3. A variable-geometry wing was still expected to offer the best solution. Total F-X costs were estimated at $7.183 billion, including $615 million for development, $4.1 billion for procurement, and $2.468 billion for operations and maintenance over a five-year period. Based on a 1,000 aircraft procurement, the average F-X flyaway cost was computed at $2.84 million per copy in FY67 dollars.

During this study the industry vacillated between a large, twin-engine aircraft with advanced radar and long-range missiles and a small, MiG-21-sized, single-engine aircraft with minimal electronics but with an emphasis on high maneuverability. Much of this was based on continuing lobbying by Boyd and his supporters, who wanted a small light-weight aircraft. However, remembering the Air Force's unhappy experience with the Lockheed F-104A Starfighter, a single-engine high-performance aircraft with minimal electronics, most contractors opted for the larger aircraft. Neither the Air Force nor the contractors seemed interested in questioning whether it had been the F-104 or the Air Force's tactics that had been the problem (it had been some of both).

The results of this Concept Formulation Study were used to prepare the F-X Development Concept Paper, which was the final step in the concept formulation phase. This paper described the F-X as a "… single-seat, twin-engine aircraft featuring excellent pilot visibility, with internal fuel sized for

a 260 nm design mission, and … a balanced combination of standoff and close-in target kill potential." The decision to include just one crew member was arrived at as much to differentiate the aircraft from the Navy's VFX (F-14A) as to save the estimated 5,000 pounds in additional structure and systems. The twin engine design was selected because it featured faster throttle response and earlier availability (interestingly, safety does not seem to have been a factor).

In a letter dated 12 September 1968, Aeronautical Systems Division Director of Engineering Standards, R. F. Semler, requested a designation for the proposed new fighter. The Navy had earlier rejected the next available fighter desig-

The 3/8th scale models were flown by NASA/Dryden to verify the basic handling qualities of the F-15 prior to and during its flight test program. The models were not fitted with wheels, and used either skids or parachutes for recovery. When parachutes were used, the models were recovered in midair by either Air Force or Navy helicopters. (NASA/Dryden)

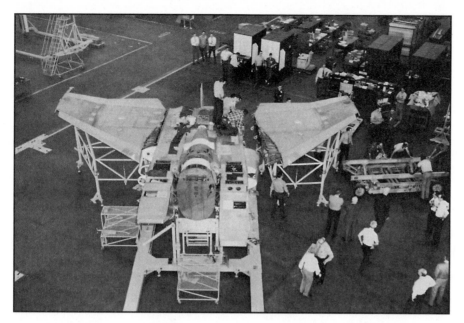

The first F-15A (71-0280) undergoes final assembly at St. Louis. Here the wings are being mated to the center fuselage section. The forward fuselage has not been attached yet. (McDonnell Douglas)

- a wing with low loading and optimized for buffet free performance at Mach 0.9,

- a high (1:1) thrust-to-weight ratio,

- a long ferry range, i.e.; to Europe without aerial refueling,

- a one man cockpit and weapon system,

- a fatigue life of 4,000 flight hours under normal fighter operations,

- a low maintenance man hours per flight hour ratio of 11.3:1,

- 360 degree visibility from the cockpit,

- self-contained engine starting with no ground support equipment required,

- a maximum gross take-off weight of 40,000 pounds for the air-superiority mission,

nation (F-13) in favor of F-14 for its VFX. With superstition also apparently influencing the Air Force, Semler declined F-13 and requested F-15 instead. The F-X now had a designation.

The RFP for the F-15 development contract was released on 30 September 1968 to Boeing, Fairchild-Republic, General Dynamics, Grumman, Lockheed, McDonnell Douglas, Northrop, and North American. Only four of the companies submitted proposals, and on 30 December three of them, McDonnell Douglas, North American, and Fairchild-Republic,

were awarded $15.4 million contracts for the Project Definition Phase. Here, each contractor would define his best F-X design with the technical proposals due on 30 June 1969, and cost proposals following two months later. The RFP gave the particulars for what the Air Force was looking for:

The F-15 markings on the second TF-15A (71-0291). The same markings were also on the vertical stabilizer. Noteworthy is the F-14 "zap" under the McDonnell Douglas name, fairly common during the F-14-versus-F-15 controversy in the early 1970s. This stylized F-15 logo was originally painted on the first aircraft (71-0280), the eighth test aircraft (71-0287), and this aircraft. It was later applied to several test aircraft that were repainted for use as ground trainers. (Dennis R. Jenkins)

- a maximum speed of Mach 2.5,

- a long range pulse-Doppler radar with look-down/shoot-down capability, and

- low development risk.

The proposals were reviewed by the F-15 System Program Office headed by BrigGen-designee Benjamin N. Bellis. One of Bellis' functions was to chair the Source Selection Evaluation Board (SSEB) that evaluated the three proposals. Eighty-seven separate factors under four major categories (technology, logistics, operations, and management) were considered, and the SSEB's ratings were forwarded, without recommendation, to the Source Selection Advisory Council (SSAC). MajGen. Lee V. Cossick chaired the SSAC and used a set of weighting factors and evaluation criteria that had been established on 2 June 1969 to evaluate the SSEB's ratings. All of this data, along with the SSAC's recommendation, was forwarded to the Secretary of the Air Force, Robert C. Seamans, Jr.

The award of the F-15 development and production contract to the McDonnell Aircraft Company division of McDonnell Douglas Corporation was announced on 23 December 1969. The McDonnell model number 199B was the result of 2.5 million man-hours of effort that had culminated in a 37,500 page proposal. And F-X now had a name—Eagle.

The terms, conditions, and restrictions of contract number F33657-70-0300 were spelled out in a 146 page document that was signed on 2 January 1970. It combined a cost-plus-incentive-fee with a fixed-price-incentive-with-successive-target arrangement which had three major items. The first item, which was the only cost-plus portion, covered engineering and design of the aircraft, its tooling, and most

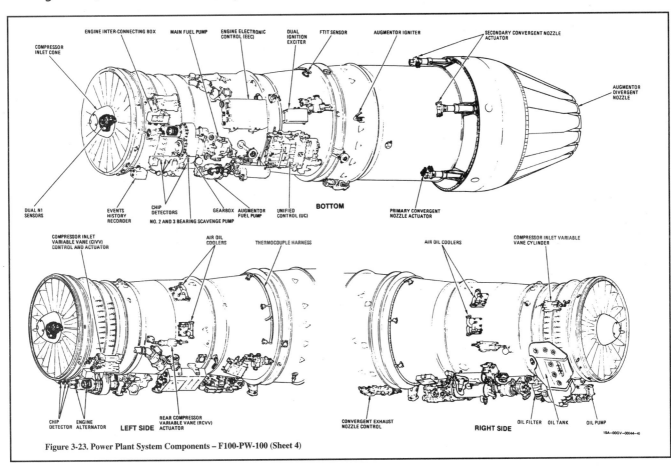

Figure 3-23. Power Plant System Components – F100-PW-100 (Sheet 4)

All F-15s have, so far, used the Pratt & Whitney F100 turbofan engine that provides 23,000 pounds of thrust in afterburner. Although initially a fairly troublesome engine, the introduction of digital electronic engine controls has allowed it to perform well in the twin-engine F-15. However, it was felt that the GE F110 engine was more reliable, and this engine has been used in most later single-engine F-16s. The F-15E is capable of using the F110 engines, although no operational aircraft have done so to date. (U.S. Air Force)

ground testing. This item had a target cost of $588 million and a maximum $47 million incentive fee. The first fixed-price item included the production of 20 Category I and II test aircraft and three static-test airframes, with a target cost of $469 million and a $42 million incentive fee. The second fixed-price item covered the first 107 operational aircraft, and was budgeted at $646 million with a $58 million incentive fee and envisioned the eventual production of 749 aircraft.

Early on, the McDonnell Douglas team had rejected variable-geometry wings as too complex, too heavy, and too expensive. The team selected instead a large fixed-geometry wing with a leading edge sweep of 45 degrees. This wing reversed a trend for fighters to have increasingly complex wings, and the F-15 had none of the slats, spoilers, slots, or other high-lift devices found on the F-4E, F-14, or other contemporary fighters. The use of advanced avionics and electronics made a single-seat configuration possible. A pair of Pratt & Whitney (P&W) afterburning turbofans were fed by large, multi-geometry, lateral intakes that, in addition to providing clean air to the engines, acted as canard surfaces, providing additional lift and maneuverability in certain flight regimes. Two gracefully swept-back vertical stabilizers and ventral fins on the bottom of the engine nacelles provided stability.

Starting in March 1970, NASA conducted an early independent evaluation of the McDonnell Douglas design and found the F-15's subsonic drag higher than predicted by McDonnell Douglas. To correct this, designers removed the ventral fins and enlarged the vertical stabilizers, along with altering their shape to be taller and less swept. These changes produced the desired drag level and also slightly enhanced stability. The airframe critical design review (CDR) was successfully accomplished in April 1971, and showed a design that differed from the proposal with horizontal tail surfaces and wings moved five inches aft to improve aircraft balance, redesigned engine air intakes, and a more symmetrical nose radome to enhance radar performance. The CDR package proposed an initial production rate of one aircraft bimonthly, increasing to one aircraft per month as the production staff acquired the necessary skills and experience to step-up to that rate with no increase in hours worked. It was planned to step-up to a maximum production rate of 12 aircraft per month.

The Air Force had decided early during conceptual development that the new fighter would employ a cannon and short-range missiles as its primary armament. This reflected a lesson-learned from the F-4, where early versions were not equipped with a cannon, much to its detriment in the skies over Vietnam. Several studies indicated that a new cannon, using caseless ammunition, could be developed that would significantly improve the F-15's kill probability, despite the technical problems previously encountered with caseless ammunition. The perceived benefits were a less complicated firing cycle since there were no empty cases to remove, and the ability to carry more rounds for a given weight since there were no heavy brass cases. In mid-1968 contracts were awarded to Gen-

The F-15 reversed a trend in fighter wing design, and has a simple wing design that only has two-position flaps and an aileron on each side. Both of the major external changes effected during the early test program are seen here (on 71-0287). The raked wingtips cured a minor buffeting problem, while the dogtooth in the horizontal stabilizer fixed a flutter condition. (NASA/Dryden)

eral Electric and Philco-Ford for the development of a new 25MM cannon. After initial proof-of-concept testing, on 21 December 1971 Philco-Ford was selected to begin detailed development of the GAU-7A cannon with a $36,181,418 three year contract for 10 cannon and 160,000 rounds of ammunition. Technical problems with the ammunition caused the Air Force to abandon the project in November 1972, and subsequently the GE M61A1 Vulcan 20MM cannon was selected as the F-15's internal armament, although provisions for the 25MM cannon exist in all airframes except the F-15E.

The Pratt & Whitney F100 afterburning turbofan was a pacing item in the F-15's development. This second-generation turbofan engine was meant to correct the multitude of problems encountered with the TF30 engine used in the F-111, but never truly lived up to its promise until the advent of digital electronic engine controls. Here, the NASA HIDEC testbed (71-0287) shows why the danger area extends over 200 feet behind the aircraft during engine run-ups. (NASA/Dryden)

Missiles had not enjoyed a good reputation among fighter pilots during the 1970s, primarily because they had not worked as advertised. During use in Southeast Asia, only 18 percent of the AIM-9s fired hit their targets, while the success rate for the AIM-7 was even worse, at 9 percent. In March 1970, General Dynamics, Hughes, and Philco-Ford received contracts for the competitive development of the XAIM-82A short-range dogfight missile to arm the F-15. By September, rising costs, political pressures, and budgetary restrictions had forced the Air Force to cancel the contracts and fall back to improved versions of the AIM-7 and AIM-9 as the F-15's primary armament. Even in the mid-1990s the United States is struggling with developing a replacement for the AIM-9, although the long-awaited AIM-120 medium-range missile is finally replacing the AIM-7.

The F-15 followed the lead established by the Navy's F-14 Tomcat, and no prototype was ordered, the initial production units being used for service trials. This raised quite a bit of controversy, many people fearing another cost overrun debacle similar to the C-5A and F-111 programs. However, for the F-15 program, the Air Force specified a set of demonstration milestones which McDonnell Douglas had to meet before the next funding allocation could be released beginning with the preliminary design review

So far the P&W F100 has powered every F-15 built, even though the Strike Eagle and its variants are capable of using the GE F110. Here a technician at Pratt's Florida facility performs checks on one of the pre-production YF100 engines scheduled for the F-15 test program. (Pratt & Whitney)

which was to be held by September 1970, and ending with a requirement that the first aircraft was to be delivered to the Air Force in November 1974.

The new F100 afterburning turbofan for the F-15 was developed largely from the P&W JTF16 demonstrator engine of the mid-1960s. P&W had to adhere to two major technical milestones: the preliminary flight rating test, which was completed in February 1972; and the final qualification test, which was completed under some controversy in May 1973. The first milestone cleared the engine for use during flight tests, while the second demonstrated its suitability

for operational use. The F100 final qualification test is the only milestone the F-15 program failed to meet on time, the original schedule calling for test completion in February 1973. During this test, the F100 was supposed to run for 150 hours at various simulated altitudes and Mach numbers, but in February 1973, seven months after the F-15 had started flying, the test engine threw a fan blade which destroyed the fan section.

Nevertheless, in March the Air Force approved the production of initial F100s conditional on meeting the 150 hour milestone by May 1973. In an attempt to ensure P&W would meet the May date, Gen. Bel-

lis deferred the high-Mach and high-altitude portions of the endurance test since it was not envisioned that the F-15 would ever actually operate at high Mach numbers or high altitude. However, the decision caused quite a commotion within Congress, and nearly caused the entire F-15 program to be cancelled.

The engine eventually passed the complete, unmodified, endurance test on 12 October 1973. The cause of the original failure was traced to a minor manufacturing defect in the prototype engine, plus some undetected rust contamination in the test chamber that had flaked off the walls and was ingested into the engine. The engine would, however, continue to be a source of problems for the F-15, and eventually the F-16.

One of the more unusual aspects of the Eagle development program was the use of three large 3/8-scale models of the F-15 which were dropped from a NASA-operated NB-52B (52-0008) at the NASA Dryden Flight Research Center. The 23.8-foot long models were constructed of aluminum, wood, and fiberglass and weighed 2,425 pounds. During the drops, the models were under radio control from the ground and were directed through high angle of attack, stalling and spinning maneuvers. At the end of the eight minute flights, the models either deployed a parachute and were recovered in midair by a helicopter, or used skid-type landing gear to land on the lakebed. One of these models, designated the "Spin Research Vehicle," served with Dryden for many years after its F-15 duties were concluded.

In an attempt to avoid some of the inlet distortion problems that had plagued the F-111 program, the F-15 inlet spent considerable time in wind tunnels at the USAF Arnold Engineering Development Center. The inlets were run both with and without engines installed, and the resulting configuration was decidedly simple for a Mach 2.5 fighter. (U.S. Air Force)

WARBIRDTECH
S E R I E S

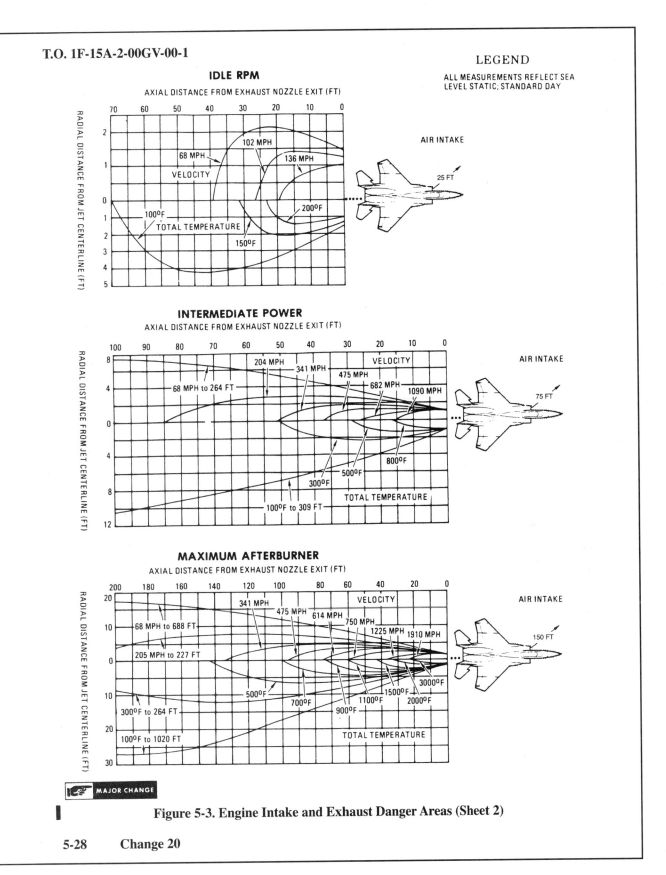

Figure 5-3. Engine Intake and Exhaust Danger Areas (Sheet 2)

The sheer power provided by the two P&W F100 engines is well illustrated by this chart showing danger areas around the aircraft. At full afterburner, the exhaust exiting the engines is traveling at 1,910 MPH and is 3,000°F! Even at engine idle, the exhaust is traveling 136 MPH and is 200°F. (U.S. Air Force)

McDONNELL DOUGLAS
F-15 EAGLE

EAGLE 2 IS BORN

This was the initial operational configuration, with 384 F-15As and 61 F-15Bs being built, including foreign military sales to Israel. There were no XF-15 or YF-15 types, all Eagles being considered "production" aircraft. The initial F-15 contract called for 20 Full Scale Development aircraft consisting of ten single-seat F-15A (71-0280/0289) and a pair of two-seat TF-15A (71-0290/0291) Category I versions, plus eight single-seat (72-0113/0120) Category II test aircraft.

Category I flight tests were carried out by McDonnell Douglas test pilots, while Category II testing was conducted by the USAF F-15 Joint Test Force. The unit later changed its title to F-15 Combined Test Force, and as of mid-1997 supports continued F-15 flight testing. Category III testing was the Follow-On Test and Evaluation, initially conducted by the Air Force Test and Evaluation Center, and later by the 433rd Fighter Weapons Squadron.

The TF-15A is dimensionally identical to the F-15A, and differs primarily in having a second seat and being 800 pounds heavier. In order to accommodate the second seat, provisions for the ALQ-135 ECM

(Above) The first F-15A (71-0280) at its roll-out ceremony in St. Louis on 26 June 1972. The aircraft was air-superiority blue, with unique markings on the forward fuselage and vertical stabilizers. The overall white missiles were dummies, and no wing pylons were carried. Like most of the test aircraft, the main and nose wheels were black. The aircraft was later partially disassembled and shipped to Edwards AFB in a C-5A transport. (McDonnell Douglas via Jack Morris)

The second F-15A (71-0281) arrives at Edwards AFB from McAir in St. Louis. The first two aircraft were disassembled and shipped in C-5As then reassembled at Edwards. Only four major components were removed—the two wings and the two horizontal stabilizers, although various minor systems were also removed, including the mass balancers on top of the vertical stabilizers. Noteworthy is that the day-glo orange markings were applied in St. Louis. (US Air Force via Jack Morris)

system was deleted and the rear of the canopy bulged slightly. The first TF-15A (71-0290, also called T1) was manufactured between the seventh and eighth single-seat aircraft, and every seventh F-15 has been a two-seater. The TF-15A was redesignated F-15B in October 1978, acknowledging the combat capabilities of the aircraft.

The first F-15A (71-0280, or F1) was rolled out during a ceremony at St. Louis on 26 June 1972. It was later partially disassembled, loaded aboard a C-5A, and transported to Edwards AFB in California, where it made its first flight on 27 July 1972 with company test pilot Irving Burrows at the controls. During this 50 minute flight the aircraft reached 12,000 feet and 320 MPH. Within the first week, the prototype had made four additional flights, totaling 4 hours and 48 minutes at speeds up to Mach 1.5 and 45,000 feet. In the next two months, Burrows and Pete Garrison would accumulate over 40 hours in 71-0280. Flight number 1,000 occurred during August 1973, by which time the F-15 had flown above 60,000 feet and at speeds in excess of Mach 2.3.

Remarkably, very few problems were encountered during the flight test program. The most serious of these, a wing buffeting problem in a small, but critical, part of the envelope (30,000 feet at Mach 0.9 and 6g) was discovered early, and engineers at St. Louis tried several fixes, most notably large fences mounted mid-span on each wing of 71-0288. The final solution was found by engineers at Edwards in March 1974, who somewhat unceremoniously sawed three

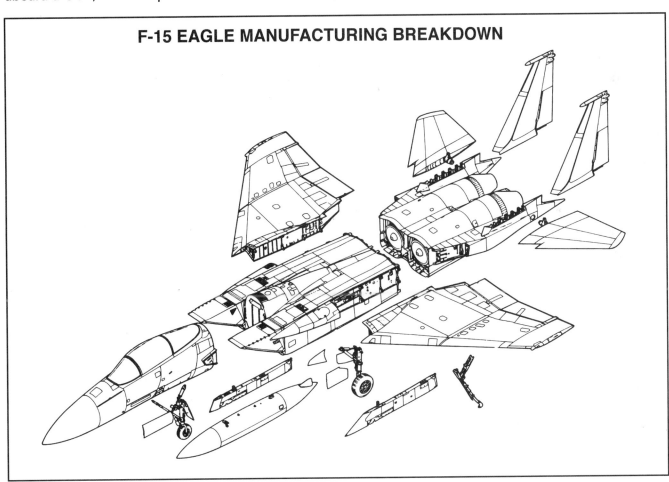

F-15 EAGLE MANUFACTURING BREAKDOWN

The manufacturing breakdown for the F-15 shows the major components that make up every variant of the Eagle. The F-15 was designed from the beginning to be easier to manufacture than the F-4. It worked: the first operational F-15A (the 21st aircraft) required 69,000 manufacturing man-hours, and an additional 11,000 man-hours in final assembly. By contrast, the first production F-4 (the 48th aircraft) had required 589,000 manufacturing man-hours and 35,000 man-hours in final assembly. For the F-15E, McDonnell Douglas redesigned the aft fuselage and most of the forward fuselage to enable the "Mud Hen" to use either P&W F100 or GE F110 engines, and to become the first two-seater to carry the ALQ-135 electronic countermeasures system. (McDonnell Douglas)

Before the world tour, the second TF-15A (71-0291) was painted to celebrate the American Bicentennial. Here, the left engine is missing its "turkey feathers" while the right engine has its full complement. This was not unusual during the mid-to-late 1970s, when maintenance crews were still struggling with making the F100 a reliable powerplant. Later, most engines simply omitted the turkey feathers altogether. Note the placement of the serial number on the bottom rear of the vertical stabilizer, compared to its placement on the world tour. (Dennis R. Jenkins)

Upon completion of its test duties, the first F-15A (71-0280) was released to the Air Force Recruiting Service for use as an attraction. The aircraft was fairly faithfully restored to its roll-out configuration although the "USAF" is a little too large and the "McDonnell Douglas" is missing from the forward fuselage. The exhibit was trucked around the country as a recruiting aid, and is shown here in Alhambra, California, during September 1979. (Dave Begy)

square feet off of each of 71-0283's wings to create the present raked wing tip. The rough edge of the wing tip was filled with wood and wood filler until metal wing tips could be fabricated. After the fix was verified, the other prototypes were similarly modified. A flutter problem discovered during wind tunnel testing resulted in a dogtooth being cut into the leading edge of the horizontal stabilizer. Later in the test program, the dorsal speed brake was found to cause excessive buffeting when it was deployed to the fully-open position. The solution was to increase its area from 20 to 31 square feet and change its shape slightly so that the required drag could be achieved with lower extension angles. These are the only major external modifications made to the F-15 during its entire 25-year production run.

The second TF-15A (71-0291, or T2) was retained by McDonnell Douglas for use as a demonstration aircraft. The aircraft was frequently shown to various potential foreign customers, and for a short period even sported French Air Force markings during an attempt to sell the F-15 to France. T2 was later given a red-white-and-blue Bicentennial color scheme in 1976 and undertook an around-the-world sales tour including

The third test aircraft sported a shark mouth in November 1977 while it was testing the Advanced Environmental Control System. An AECS logo is barely visible on the air intake behind the drop tank, and an Eagle logo is on the tail. Also unusual are the extra formation light strips on the vertical stabilizers. The lights were on the left side of both tails, but there were none on the right side of either tail. There were also additional formation light strips on the upper wing surfaces. (Dennis R. Jenkins)

The eighth test aircraft (71-0287) was delivered in a gloss white paint scheme to assist in photography during spin tests, although day-glo orange was added for increased visibility. A spin parachute was installed above the engines to aid in recovery after departure from controlled flight. Thanks largely to work accomplished by NASA with the 3/8th scale model program, the spin characteristics of the F-15 were fairly benign. This aircraft was later bailed to NASA/Dryden. 71-0287 was one of three test aircraft that routinely had the "F-15" markings on the nose and tail. (Dennis R. Jenkins)

The view of an F-15 from a KC-135. This was an early test aircraft which still has the original (unclipped) wing tips. The dog-toothed horizontal stabilizer has already been added however. The refueling receptacle is behind the pilot's line of sight, but the pilot can visually confirm boom contact if required, unlike most other fighters where the receptacle is totally out of sight. (Don Logan)

An early Luke F-15A (74-0117) shows the clean lines of the Eagle. The left fin cap is missing the rounded rear radome for the ALQ-128 antenna. The normal ALQ-135 antennas are also missing from the forward fuselage. Development and integration of both ECM systems lagged behind, and most early F-15s were delivered with little or no ECM capability. The ALQ-135 system development and integration would not be complete until 1996, 21 years after the system was first fielded on the F-15A. (Roger Smith)

a stop at the Farnborough air show in Britain. This aircraft was also used to demonstrate various advanced concepts, including Wild Weasel and reconnaissance variants. In later years, 71-0291 served as the F-15E Strike Eagle demonstrator and was used to test the conformal fuel tank concept.

Production of the initial batch of 30 F-15A/B operational aircraft commenced in March 1973. The first operational Eagle to be delivered was a TF-15A (73-0108, named TAC-1) formally accepted by the 555th Tactical Fighter Training Squadron of the 58th Tactical Training Wing at Luke AFB, Arizona, on 4 November 1974 in a ceremony presided over by President Gerald Ford.

The F-15 flight test program generated 38 engineering change proposals, compared to the 135 generated by the F-4 Phantom II. All but two of these were incorporated into the first operational aircraft (73-0108), and all were incorporated into the third (73-0085). All aircraft designs seem to increase in empty (dry) weight prior to and during production, with the original F-4 gaining 3,050 pounds between the first prototype and

One of the early F-15As (73-0089) receives a new engine on the flight line at Luke AFB. The F-15 was designed to make engine changes easier than they had been in the F-4. This was demonstrated when a McDonnell Douglas team changed a complete F100 in just under 19 minutes. Since data indicated that the engine required replacement more often than the accessories, most major accessories are mounted on the airframe and powered by a common drive system instead of being attached to the engine. (Dennis R. Jenkins)

The commander of the 58th TFTW painted an TF-15A (73-0111) with multi-colored stripes on each rudder, providing one of the few spots of color on early F-15s at Luke. The first 30 operational aircraft were fitted with a speed brake made of graphite-epoxy that required an external stiffener on the top of the speed brake. Improvements in the manufacture of the speed brake allowed the external stiffener to be deleted beginning with block-10 aircraft. (Mick Roth)

The F-15 is actually old enough to have taken on fuel from propeller-driven tankers. Here a 57th FWW F-15A (73-0087) takes on fuel from an Arizona Air Guard KC-97L (53-0244) in the skies near Luke AFB. Noteworthy is that the F-15's speed brake is at almost full extension in an attempt to maintain a sufficiently slow speed. Pilots generally preferred to receive fuel from KC-135 (and later KC-10) aircraft since the refueling speeds were more in line with the Eagle's flight regime. (U.S. Air Force)

The F-15 was introduced to operational service in a ceremony at Luke AFB on 14 November 1974. The first operational aircraft was a TF-15A (73-0108) named "TAC-1," and was dedicated by President Gerald Ford. The aircraft was air-superiority blue, and did not carry tail codes yet. Like most of the air-superiority blue aircraft, the refueling receptacle door was painted a dark gray. Two TF-15As actually arrived at Luke on the same day, but the second (73-0109) was not presented to the public, and did not have a name. (Dennis R. Jenkins)

An F-15A (74-0117) from the 555th TFTS begins a slow descent over the Arizona desert in August 1976. The clipped wing tips and dogtooth horizontal stabilizer show up well in this view, as do the large unpainted areas of the rear fuselage. The square outline on the bottom of the external tank shows ground crews where to position the loading cart under the tank. The "eagle claws" that secure the Sparrow missiles are visible at each fuselage missile station. These adapters were changed slightly to accommodate the AIM-120 missile when it was introduced in the 1990s. (Roger Smith)

The first Compass Ghost aircraft (73-0100) shows the upper surface paint scheme. Small walkways are painted on the horizontal stabilizer. The gun exhaust grills are normally painted gray, but this quickly turns to black after the cannon has been fired a few times. Late in the F-15A production run, the top center of the fuselage, directly behind the speed brake, was slightly reshaped to simplify manufacture. (McDonnell Douglas)

the first production aircraft. In contrast, the F-15 gained only 188 pounds. And, in fact, between the third operational aircraft and the 87th (74-0117), weight was down 283 pounds.

The F-15 was designed from the start to be easier and faster to produce than previous fighters with the use of large one piece forgings instead of building-up many smaller pieces.

The Air Force had estimat-

After the test program was completed, several of the early test aircraft received new gloss white paint jobs with a contrasting trim color. Here the fourth F-15A (71-0283) has bright orange (but not day-glo) trim. 71-0285, 71-0289, and 71-0290 used royal blue trim in the same general scheme. The aircraft were used for training maintenance and ground crews, and many reports show they were redesignated GF-15A, although official records do not confirm this. (Dennis R. Jenkins)

The F-15 was designed to be easier to maintain than previous fighters. Three large panels open around each engine to provide maintenance access, and the engine is removed as a unit with less disassembly than required on previous fighters. However, much of the work still needs to be accomplished from below, and the aft fuselage is fairly close to the ground, forcing some contortions on the part of maintenance personnel. The augmentor fuel drains protruded a couple of inches beneath the aft fuselage and frequently ground personnel were injured by hitting them while working under the aircraft. In the mid-1990s the protrusions were finally removed. (Dennis R. Jenkins)

The cockpit of the F-15A still used conventional instrumentation although MSIP added a multi-function armament panel. This was an early test aircraft, and has some additional instrumentation in the upper right position normally occupied by the TEWS ECM display. (Dennis R. Jenkins)

ed needing 690,000 manufacturing man-hours for the first five aircraft, but McDonnell Douglas completed them in only 466,000 man-hours. The first operational F-15A required 69,000 manufacturing man-hours, and an additional 11,000 man-hours in final assembly. By contrast, the first production F-4 (the 48th aircraft) had required 589,000 manufacturing man-hours and 35,000 man-hours in final assembly.

One of the F-15 contract requirements was the ability to change an engine in less than 30 minutes. After a fair amount of practice, a highly choreographed McDonnell Douglas team met this requirement by changing a

Remarkably, very few problems were encountered during the flight test program. However, a wing buffeting problem at altitudes around 30,000 feet at Mach 0.9 and 6g was discovered and engineers in St. Louis tried several fixes, most notably large fences mounted mid-span on each wing of 71-0288 (above). The final solution was found by engineers at Edwards in March 1974, who somewhat unceremoniously sawed off three square feet of each of 71-0283's wings to create the present raked wing tip. (McDonnell Douglas)

The center fuselage appears as a rectangular housing for fuel tanks and the air intakes (the two tunnels visible here). The next step is for the wings and aft fuselage to be joined. Later the forward fuselage is attached. (McDonnell Douglas)

A forward view of the center fuselage shows the area that the M61 20MM cannon will occupy. The fixed part of the inlet is also visible. Assembly is still manpower intensive, although most of the actual fabrication of the metal pieces is automated. (McDonnell Douglas)

complete engine assembly in 18 minutes and 55 seconds on 12 February 1974. The company readily admitted that the average Air Force unit probably could not duplicate this feat (although, in fact, several have including an ANG unit), but the demonstration fulfilled the contract requirement, and proved the F-15 could be quickly serviced. An unintentional, but welcome, feature introduced on the F-15 was reduced noise. As measured one mile from the departure end of a runway, the F-15 is 15 decibels quieter than the F-4, and 13 decibels quieter than the F-104.

Titanium bulkheads are milled four at a time by a machine controlled by the same computer system that houses the CAD/CAM design for the F-15. This ensures that the latest engineering is used in the construction of the aircraft, and saves considerable time setting up the automated milling machines. (McDonnell Douglas)

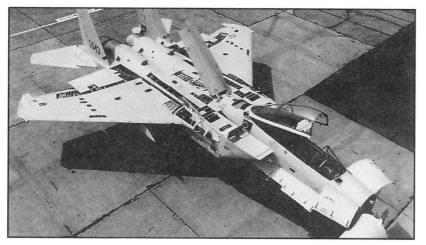

(Above) The ACES II ejection seat used in most later F-15s, and also fitted to the General Dynamics (Lockheed) F-16. This is a zero-zero seat, meaning it can successfully eject a pilot from an aircraft sitting on the parking ramp. It takes just five seconds from the initiation of ejection to full parachute deployment. Until the fall of the Soviet Union, the USAF was certain it had the best ejection seats in the world. Subsequent evaluation of Russian designs revealed that their seats were superior in many ways, and have resulted in various modifications to USAF seats. (McDonnell Douglas)

McDonnell Douglas staged this publicity shot to illustrate the number of access panels in the F-15. Most of these can be used by maintenance personnel without the need for special stands since they can be reached from the ground or from on top of the aircraft. All major components can be reached without removing other components. (McDonnell Douglas)

FOR THE RECORD

THE DAY THE EAGLE STREAKED

Beginning on 16 January 1975, three Air Force pilots and a modified F-15A made an assault on the world class time-to-climb records for aircraft powered by jet engines. The three pilots, Maj. Roger Smith, Maj. W. R. 'Mac" Macfarlane, and Maj. Dave Peterson were all members of the F-15 Joint Test Force at Edwards. Pete Garrison, a McDonnell Douglas test pilot, was instrumental in the development of the flight profiles used for the record flights.

On 1 April 1974, the Air Force awarded McDonnell Douglas a $2.1 million dollar contract to modify an early F-15A to support the record attempt. All existing test aircraft were evaluated, with the choice narrowed between F5 (71-0284) and F17 (72-0119). The fact that it was 800 pounds lighter than F5 and was an unneeded attrition aircraft whose absence would have little, if any, impact on the flight test program led to the final choice of 72-0119. The aircraft was modified

by deleting all non-mission critical systems including the flap and speed brake actuators, the cannon and ammunition handling equipment, the radar and fire-control systems, non-critical cockpit displays and radios, one of the generators, the utility hydraulic system, the landing lights, and, of course, the 50 pounds of paint (hence the Streak Eagle name). Additions included a revised oxygen system, support equipment for the full pressure suit worn by the pilots, extra batteries, a

Streak Eagle at Buckley ANGB, Colorado, in December 1974 on her way to Grand Forks AFB for the record runs. The metal patch over the normal ALQ-128 antenna location on the forward fuselage is evident, as is the faired over gun port in the wing root. All test aircraft fitted with the long instrumentation boom used metal noses instead of the normal composite units. Noteworthy is the 610 gallon centerline tank, which is painted air superiority blue. The weight reduction efforts went so far as to remove the landing lights from the nose landing gear strut, deemed unnecessary since all flights would be conducted during the day. (Duane Kuhn)

Streak Eagle (72-0119) returns from an early test flight. The tail badge was removed before the record runs, and reads "Aquila Maxima" (roughly, "ultimate Eagle"). Also noteworthy in this photograph is the configuration of the pods on top of the vertical stabilizers. For the record runs, these were replaced by very small mass balancers (not the normal production configuration). (McDonnell Douglas)

The various alloys used to construct the F-15 are evident in this view of Streak Eagle (72-0119). Very few composites are used by the F-15, the last major combat aircraft not to make use of the new materials. Streak Eagle carried very few markings, noticeably a national insignia (with outline) on the wing. Modifications visible in this view include the deletion of a cooling scoop on the right fuselage boom next to the engine. Interestingly, the tail hook remains completely covered by its doors, something that would later be changed on operational F-15s to ease maintenance and eliminate a small amount of weight. (U.S. Air Force)

pitot boom with alpha and beta vanes, an over-the-shoulder video camera, a battery powered radio, sensitive accelerometers, a standby attitude gyro, a large VHF antenna under the canopy behind the pilot, and a special "hold-down" device in place of the tail hook.

All of this effort resulted in saving approximately 1,800 pounds. When weighed in preparation for a 30,000 meter run (on test flight #37), 72-0119 weighed 36,799 pounds.

For the record attempts the aircraft was physically held-down to the runway while full power was applied.

The record runs were accomplished at Grand Forks AFB, North Dakota, where the cold atmospheric conditions were ideal. Six different record flights were flown (there were several unsuccessful ones in between), and margins of between 15 and 33 percent were achieved over the previous records.

A highly modified MiG-25 (E-266) later recaptured several of the higher altitude records, and also set one to 35,000 meters, although it is still a matter of some controversy over whether it was rocket assisted. All of these records have since been broken by the P-42 prototype for the Sukhoi Su-27 fighter. There was consideration given to further modifying Streak Eagle, including using more powerful production engines, and making another attempt, but this never material-

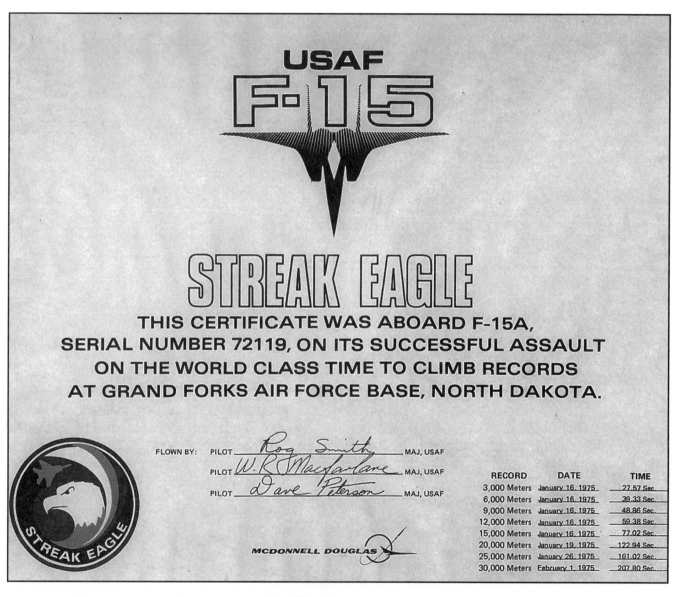

RECORD	DATE	TIME
3,000 Meters	January 16, 1975	27.57 Sec.
6,000 Meters	January 16, 1975	39.33 Sec.
9,000 Meters	January 16, 1975	48.86 Sec.
12,000 Meters	January 16, 1975	59.38 Sec.
15,000 Meters	January 16, 1975	77.02 Sec.
20,000 Meters	January 19, 1975	122.94 Sec.
25,000 Meters	January 26, 1975	161.02 Sec.
30,000 Meters	February 1, 1975	207.80 Sec.

Certificates like this one were carried aboard Streak Eagle during its record flights, one of its few non-essential pay-loads. The record data was filled in after the record flights were completed. The certificates were later given to friends of the pilots, dignitaries, and company officials. (Dennis R. Jenkins Collection, with many thanks to Roger Smith)

STREAK EAGLE RECORDS

ALTITUDE (METERS)	DATE	PILOT	OLD RECORD (SECONDS)	GOAL (SECONDS)	ACTUAL (SECONDS)
3,000	16 Jan 75	Smith	34.50	27.00	27.57
6,000	16 Jan 75	Macfarlane	48.80	38.60	39.33
9,000	16 Jan 75	Macfarlane	61.70	47.90	48.86
12,000	16 Jan 75	Macfarlane	77.10	58.00	59.38
15,000	16 Jan 75	Peterson	114.50	73.70	77.02
20,000	19 Jan 75	Smith	169.80	126.10	122.94
25,000	26 Jan 75	Peterson	192.60	163.70	161.02
30,000	01 Feb 75	Smith	243.90	206.90	207.80

ized. Streak Eagle has since been turned over to the Air Force Museum where, to protect it from corrosion, it has been painted in a Compass Ghost scheme utilizing two tones of blue instead of the normal gray. The museum's plans for the aircraft are uncertain, management preferring to obtain an operational F-15C (preferably a MiG killer) and discard Streak Eagle.

Streak Eagle (72-0119) getting ready for a test flight at Grand Forks AFB, North Dakota. Besides the lack of paint, other external changes included modified mass balancers on top of each vertical stabilizer, and a long instrumentation boom on the nose. Note the large UHF antenna under the rear of the canopy. Weight reduction efforts included removing all military equipment (cannon, ammunition handling, radar, fire control, etc.) along with the flap and speed brake actuators. (Doug Slowiak via the Jay Miller Collection)

TEETHING 4 PROBLEMS

Deliveries of the first operational F-15A/Bs to the 1st TFW at Langley AFB, began in January 1976, replacing F-4Es. Although by all accounts smooth for a new fighter, the introduction of the F-15 into service was not without its problems. The first squadrons found that they could not mount the planned number of sorties because of various minor maintenance problems, but the most serious concern was the engines. The F100 had numerous teething troubles, which should have been expected for such a new and advanced engine.

The F-15 was the first of a new generation of highly-maneuverable fighters, and the Air Force had grossly underestimated the number of engine power cycles per sortie where the pilots were constantly changing throttle settings to exploit their newfound maneuverability while not overstressing their aircraft. This caused unexpectedly high wear and tear on key engine components, resulting in frequent failures of components such as first-stage turbine blades. But the most serious problem was with stagnation stalling.

Since the compressor blades of a jet engine are airfoil sections, they can stall if the angle at which the airflow strikes them exceeds a critical value, cutting off airflow into the combustion chamber. Stagnation stalls most often occurred during high angle-of-attack maneuvers, and they usually resulted in abrupt interruptions of the flow of air through the compressor. This caused the engine core to lose speed, and the turbine to overheat. If this condition was not quickly corrected, damage to the turbine could take place or a fire could occur. This was especially dangerous in a twin-engine aircraft like the F-15, since the pilot might not immediately notice that one of his engines had failed. To correct for this, an audible warning system was attached to the turbine temperature reading.

Stagnation stalls could also be caused by a "hard" afterburner start, which was the afterburner failing to light when commanded to do so by the pilot. In this case, large amounts of unburnt fuel collected in the aft end of the tailpipe, which was explosively ignited by the hot gases coming from the engine core. The pressure wave from the explosion then propagated forward to the fan, causing the fan to stall and sometimes even causing the forward compressor stage to stall as well. These types of stagnation stalls usually occurred at high altitudes and at high Mach numbers. The normal recovery technique for a stagnation stall was for the pilot to shut the engine

An F-15C (86-0150) from Mountain Home's 366th OG shows the new band-3 ALQ-135B antennas on the forward fuselage in front of the windscreen (and on the bottom fuselage) in October 1995. The antenna presents a mostly triangular shape protruding approximately two inches above the mold line. This antenna finally completes the coverage for the ALQ-135B, and has been shown in documentation since at least 1985. It has only been recently that aircraft have actually been fitted with it, however. The lack of coverage for this band has caused the ALQ-135 to be severely criticized by the Government Accounting Office (GAO) and others. As originally fielded, the ALQ-135 provided coverage for only two of the ten most widely used Soviet radars. Upgrades quickly covered others, but even during Desert Storm the system did not offer protection against all threats, and possibly contributed to the loss of one F-15E. (Mick Roth)

EXTERIOR INSPECTION

AN/ALE-45 COUNTERMEASURES

DISPENSER SET

1. (Loaded Dispenser) CMD ground safety switch pin - INSTALLED
2. Loaded Dispenser (s) - PROPERLY INSTALLED

> **CAUTION**
>
> Flares shall not be carried in the left outboard fuselage CMD station or in the outer row on the inboard fuselage CMD station when the LANTIRN Targeting pod is installed.

3. Moldline closure panels - INSTALLED

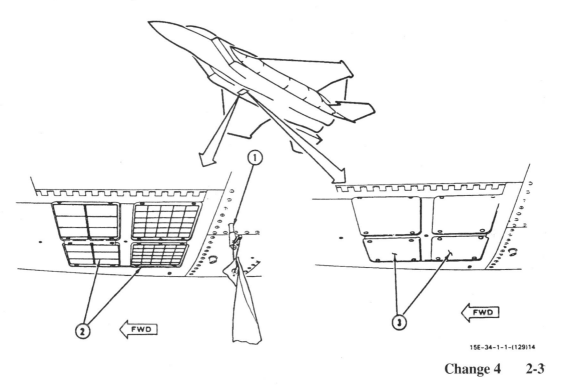

15E-34-1-1-(129)14

Change 4   2-3

Two Tracor ALE-45 expendable countermeasures dispensers are located in the bottom of the fuselage immediately forward of each main landing gear wheel well, although the system is seldom seen fitted while the aircraft are in the United States. Installation provisions exist in all F-15C/Ds, and the F-15E, but apparently initially not in USAF F-15A/Bs. However, at least some part of the wiring was incorporated into USAF F-15As, and the system control switch exists on the throttle quadrant of all F-15s. The MSIP program installed provisions for the ALE-45 into all remaining USAF F-15A/Bs. At least some Israeli F-15As are equipped with the ALE-45 dispensers or equivalent locally-produced systems. The ALE-45 is a solid-state microprocessor controlled dispenser which interfaces to ALR-56 warning system for automatic operation. The set determines the best dispensing program based on operating mode, payload management inputs, available expendables, threat type, altitude, velocity and aspect angle to the threat. The set can also be controlled manually by the pilot. The set has four dispensers, each with two magazines, and is capable of dispensing RR-170 or RR-180 chaff (240 cartridges maximum), MJU-7 flares (120 cartridges), and MJU-10 flares (48 cartridges). One-quarter of the flare load can not be carried on F-15Es when the LANTIRN targeting pod is installed. (U.S. Air Force)

Two F-15s from Kadena AB, Okinaw, fly over the Pacific Ocean. The large, uncomplicated wing gives the F-15 exceptional maneuverability, especially considering its sheer size and weight. Having an outstanding thrust-to-weight ratio did not hurt either. (U.S. Air Force)

1976 the F-15 fleet had suffered 11-12 stagnation stalls per 1,000 flying hours but by the end 1981, this rate was down to 1.5 per thousand. However, the F100 still had a reputation of being a temperamental engine under certain conditions until digital electronic engine controls were developed for the improved F100-PW-220 version.

Engine problems not withstanding, not a single F-15 was lost during the flight test program, and the F-15 is the only USAF jet fighter to complete its first 5,000 flight hours without a loss. The first F-15 loss (73-0088) occurred on 15 October 1975 after a total of 7,300 hours had been accumulated by 47 F-15s. The loss resulted from the pilot turning off both generators because he had smoke in the cockpit, resulting in a temporary loss of power to the fuel boost pumps, causing both engines to flame-out. The emergency generator came on-line, but the aircraft had been on a low level gunnery mission, and was at too low an altitude to effect

off and allow it to spool down, then attempt a restart as soon as the turbine temperature returned to a normal level. Of course, this was unacceptable in combat situations or at low altitudes.

There were frequent groundings and delays in engine deliveries while an attempt was made to fix these problems. Strikes at two major subcontractors aggravated the problem and further delayed the delivery of engines. By the end of 1979, the Air Force was forced to accept F-15 airframes and place them in storage until sufficient numbers of engines could be delivered to fly the aircraft. A massive effort by Pratt & Whitney helped alleviate this problem, but the F-15 suffered from an engine shortage for a long time.

Early problems with the reliability of the F100 engines were largely overcome by improvements in materials, maintenance, and operating procedures. The installation of a

quartz window in the side of the afterburner assembly to enable a sensor to monitor the pilot flame of the augmentor helped to cure the problem with the "hard" afterburner starts. Modifications to the fuel control system helped lower the frequency of stagnation stalls. During

This F-15C (80-0051) from the 54th TFS at Elmendorf AFB, Alaska, shows the conformal fuel tanks in their air-superiority (type-1) configuration. These tanks are optimized for carrying AIM-7 missiles instead of bombs, and were normally fitted to the Alaskan Air Command aircraft when they intercepted Soviet reconnaissance aircraft. (Mick Roth)

an air-start. The pilot ejected successfully.

The second F-15 loss (74-0129) occurred in early 1977 after 177 Eagles had accumulated over 30,000 flight hours. The aircraft collided with an aggressor F-5E during a Red Flag exercise at Nellis AFB. Compare these two losses to other jet fighter statistics at 30,000 flight hours: F-100, 26 losses; F-101, 12 losses; F-102, 20 losses; F-104, 24 losses (USAF only); F-105, 8 losses; F-106, 6 losses; F-111, 6 losses; F-4, 9 losses (USAF only); F-14, 5 losses; and the F-16 at 7 losses.

In fact, by the end of FY88, the F-15 had logged over 1 million flight hours and was averaging 3.27 major accidents per 100,000 flight hours, compared to it nearest rival, the F-16, at 6.52. This earned the F-15 the distinction of being the safest fighter in the history of the Air Force. Fifteen years earlier, from 1956 to 1973, the average loss rate

One of the high-visibility marking test aircraft from the 555th TFTS/58th TFW at Luke was this TF-15A (73-0112) in August 1976. This black-and-white stripe scheme was not identical to the red-and-white striped aircraft. The aircraft was air-superiority blue and did not have an outline around the national insignia. Black wheels were typical of early operational aircraft. (Mick Roth)

for twin-engine fighters was 10.5, while single-engine fighters had lost a staggering 17.1 per 100,000 flight hours (not including combat). By FY95, this rate was down to 1.53 major accidents per 100,000 flight hours for the F-15, with the F-16 following at 2.15.

The last of the F-15A/Bs that were built were delivered to fighter interceptor squadrons that had been absorbed by TAC when the Air Defense Command was disbanded in October 1979. Four squadrons (5th, 48th, 57th, and 318th Fighter Interceptor Squadrons) received F-15s for use in the interceptor role, replacing the Convair F-106 Delta Dart. The role of the Eagle in the air defense of the United States was a brief one, with that role now being carried out by the F-16A Fighting Falcon. The Eagle interceptor squadrons were deactivated during the early 1990s, and their aircraft were passed along to the Air National Guard.

F-15C/D

The F-15C was initially known as "PEP-2000" (Production Eagle Package), and included an additional 2,000 pounds of internal fuel, the ability to carry conformal fuel tanks (CFT), an additional UHF radio, improved ECM equipment, a strengthened airframe, and a new

A pair of F-106s Delta Darts were used as dissimilar air combat opponents for a pair of F-15As (including 77-0131). In some flight regimes the F-106 was a worthy opponent, but for the most part the F-15's superior thrust-to-weight ratio and faster turn rate made any combat a foregone conclusion. By this time, most F-15s wore black tail codes, and the standard markings included a national insignia without an outline, a squadron badge on the air intake, and a TAC badge (mostly missing here) on the tail. (U.S. Air Force)

This 48th FIS F-15C (79-0077) shows typical markings on the forward part of the aircraft. Untypical however, is the fact that it claims to be an F-15C-21-MC, when in fact it is a block-26 aircraft. Here the national insignia is a series of "dotted" lines, omitting the color used earlier in its career. Even the squadron emblem on the air intake is monochrome. Although the F-15 was equipped with a built-in boarding ladder, most crews prefer to use the larger ground-support ladder shown here. (Dennis R. Jenkins)

During April 1977, this Bitburg TF-15A (76-0125) wore no markings other than tail codes. Even for the F-15, this was plain. A simple stripe along the fin cap and a squadron badge on the air intake were added later. (Ron Picciani)

ejection seat. The additional fuel capacity raised the gross weight of the F-15C to over 68,000 pounds, and consequently, the tires, wheels, and brakes were strengthened. The F-15C/D is equipped with an overload warning system which permits the pilot to maneuver safely to the 9g limit of the airframe at all design gross weights, as opposed to the 7.33g restriction applied to the F-15A/B in certain flight regimes. As in the F-15A/B, the only significant difference between the single-seat F-15C and two-seat F-15D is the lack of some defensive electronics and a bulged canopy to cover the second crew member.

The first F-15C (78-0468) made its initial flight on 26 February 1979 in St. Louis, and the two-seat F-15D (78-0561) first flew on 19 June 1979. A total of 485 F-15Cs and 90 F-15Ds were produced, including those for USAF service and for export to Israel and Saudi Arabia. The 1,000th F-15 (84-0030) was delivered on 3 October 1986.

The only external difference between the F-15A and the F-15C was the introduction of the capability of carrying conformal fuel tanks attached to the side of

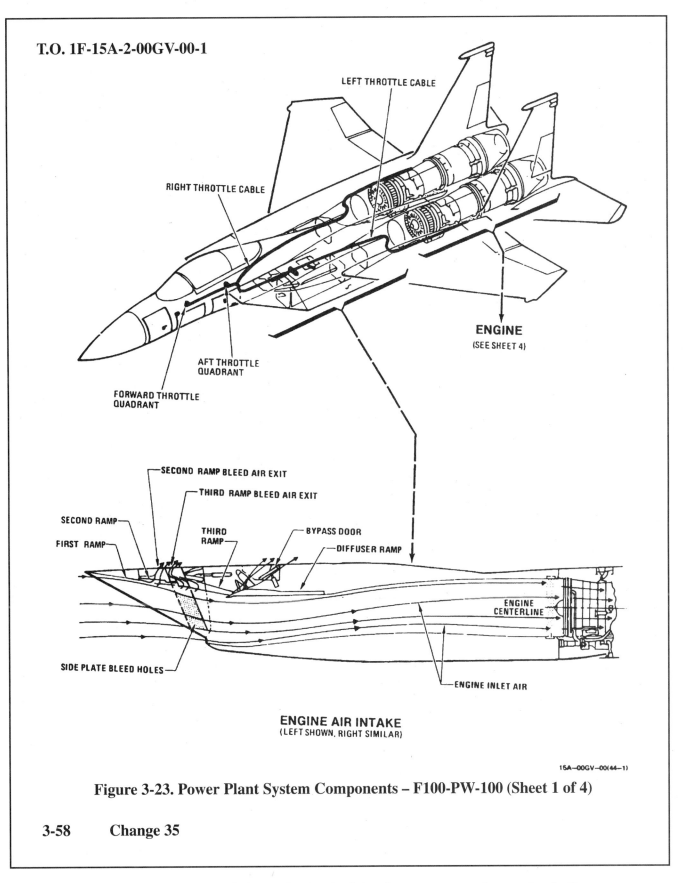

Figure 3-23. Power Plant System Components – F100-PW-100 (Sheet 1 of 4)

Compared to most other supersonic fighters, the F-15's air intake ramp system is very simple. Three ramps, two bleed air exits, and a diffuser position to keep airflow to the engine subsonic. (U.S. Air Force)

The F-15 has a severe angle of attack while landing, as shown by the first F-15C (78-0468) at Edwards AFB in October 1981. The speed brake is shown at its full extension. The air intakes and the horizontal stabilators are parallel to the runway typical of the landing configuration. The "F-15C" and photo reference markings on the forward fuselage and vertical stabilizers are unique. (Dennis R. Jenkins)

One of artist Keith Ferris' paint schemes was applied to this F-15A (74-0110) during early 1977. This bottom view of the aircraft, complete with false canopy, shows how deceptive the paint scheme could be. The landing gear being down ruins some of the effect in this photograph. An attempt was made to paint most of the rear fuselage, but paint can already be seen flaking off the left rear fuselage boom. (Mick Roth)

each air intake. During the F-X proposal effort, McDonnell Douglas had investigated the concept of conformal packs to contain fuel and other systems without taking up space on the aircraft's weapons stations in an attempt to fulfill the "transatlantic" ferry range required in the RFP. In early-1974 McDonnell Douglas decided to demonstrate the concept, dubbed "FAST (Fuel and Sensor Tactical) Pack," to the Air Force and other potential customers.

The conformal fuel tanks are designed for quick installation and are fitted to the F-15 using a standard USAF bomb lift truck with a simple adapter. Maintenance personnel raise it into position, install two bolts, and make one electrical and two fluid connections. The CFTs are not capable of being jettisoned, but the fuel can be dumped through the aircraft's normal dump system. Each CFT has a maximum cross-section of 24 by 36 inches, and the AIM-7 or AIM-120 missiles they displace can be carried on the corners of the CFT itself. In addition to fuel, McDonnell Douglas has proposed versions containing reconnaissance equipment, Wild Weasel systems, low-level strike equipment, and even one version that incorporated a rocket engine in the back that

could be used for thrust augmentation. Only the fuel-carrying version has ever been manufactured.

The prototype FAST Packs were completed just 139 days after the engineering go-ahead and first flew on the second TF-15A (71-0291) on 27 July 1974. In September 1974 the aircraft took-off weighing 67,000 pounds, including 33,000 pounds of fuel, and flew 3,063 miles from Loring AFB, Maine, to the Farnborough airshow unrefueled. Total flight time was 5.4 hours at Mach 0.85 with 4,300 pounds of fuel remaining. The design was quickly purchased by Israel for local production, and was retrofitted to the IDF/AF F-15As, making them the only operational F-15As to carry CFTs. The USAF subsequently decided to equip most F-15C/Ds with the capability to carry type-1 conformal fuel tanks, and also specified a modified tangential carriage) version (type-4) for the F-15E.

Compared to the F-15A, significant improvements were made to the electronics suite of the F-15C. An improved version of the APG-63 radar was fitted to the initial F-15Cs, but this was replaced by a significantly modified version designated APG-70 beginning in 1989. Both units are equipped with a programmable signal processor that allows much more rapid

The second TF-15A (71-0291) in August 1974 on an early test flight of the FAST Packs. Noteworthy are the large unpainted areas of the lower fuselage. This area gets very hot due to engine heating, and the paint required frequent touch-up. It was quickly decided that it was far easier to leave this area, and a smaller area on top of the fuselage, unpainted. (McDonnell Douglas)

One of the F-15Ds (84-0042) that is maintained at Edwards AFB for continued testing is shown in November, 1985. The aircraft is missing the "turkey feathers" on its engines, and is carrying both Sidewinder and Sparrow missiles. (Dennis R. Jenkins)

One of the few F-15Bs (77-0158) assigned to the 32nd TFS at Soesterberg AB, Netherlands. This squadron conducted a great many intercepts of Soviet reconnaissance aircraft during the cold war. This June 1979 shot was taken at Cold Lake, Canada. Several Soesterberg Eagles were modified with intercept lights (basically landing lights that shine sideways on the left side of the fuselage) to illuminate Soviet aircraft in the dark. (Peter Wilson)

This F-15A (76-0071) from the 71st TFS at Langley has its cannon removed for maintenance. There is remarkably little structure in this area of the wing, and little is left after the access panels are removed. The single door that normally provides access to the cannon for routine maintenance is open in this photograph. (Dennis R. Jenkins)

switching of the radar between different modes for maximum operational flexibility and paved the way for adding the synthetic aperture mode to the F-15E. The APG-70 was retrofitted to most early F-15C/Ds by the MSIP-II program, and the APG-63 in the A/Bs were upgraded using some technology developed for the new radar.

Most F-15Cs were delivered with Pratt & Whitney F100-PW-100 turbofans, but were later fitted with more reliable but slightly lower rated (maximum afterburning thrust reduced from 23,830 to 23,450 pounds) F100-PW-220 engines. This engine was first tested on an F-15A (71-0287) at Edwards in 1982, and features single-crystal turbine airfoils, an advanced multi-zone augmentor, an increased airflow fan, and, most significantly, a digital electronic engine control system. The new engine was introduced on the production line in November 1985, and began operational service in the spring 1986. For the first time, F-15 pilots could confidently slam both throttles without having to worry about the dangers of engine stagnations. During the early 1990s, improved -220E engines began to trickle into operational F-15s.

The first unit to receive F-15C/Ds was the 18th TFW at Kadena, Okinawa, during September 1979, marking the first Pacific deployment of the Eagle. Next was the 32nd TFS based at Soesterberg in the Netherlands, and with the exception of the 49th TFW at Holloman AFB, the F-15C/D replaced all F-15A/Bs in Air Force service. The F-15A/Bs were transferred to Air National Guard squadrons replacing F-4s and F-106s.

An ALQ-135B radome is mounted on the right tail boom on most F-15C/D aircraft, and on both tail booms on F-15E aircraft. A few F-15A aircraft have also been seen with the radome. The latest modification seen on a few F-15Cs changes the shape of the radome to be more of a rounded rectangle instead of perfectly round. (Dennis R. Jenkins)

The F-15's landing gear appears too fragile to handle such a large aircraft, and in fact, has been beefed up several times over the production run as the aircraft's gross weight has increased. But it has never compromised the aircraft, as the Israeli's proved when they landed one F-15A at 260 knots after it had lost most of its right wing. In the mid-1990s, the X-33 technology demonstrator program elected to use an F-15E landing gear for its Mach 15 test vehicle. One drawback to the F-15 configuration is the relatively narrow track of the main gear, making the Eagle somewhat susceptible to cross-winds while taxiing. (Michael Grove via the Mick Roth Collection)

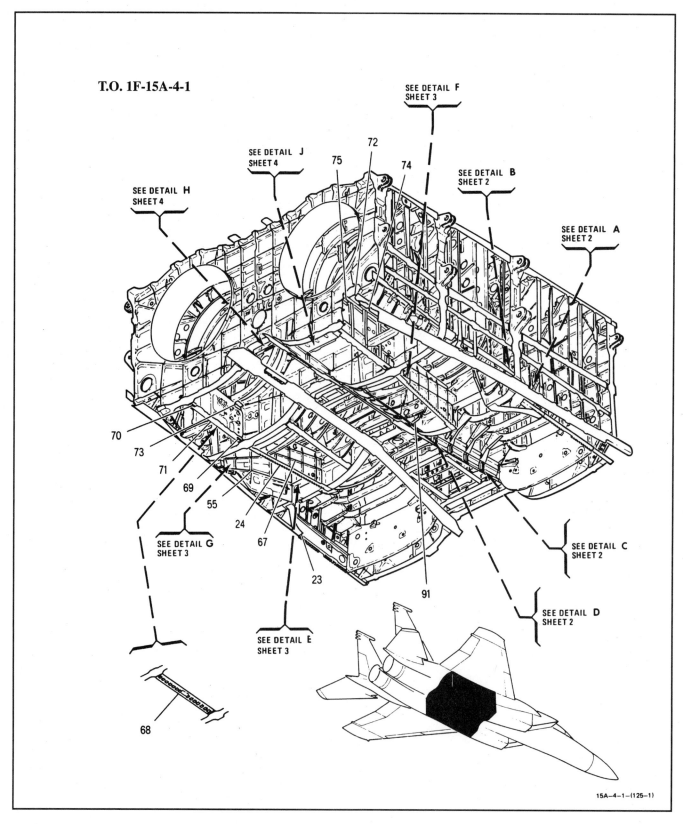

SEE DETAIL F
SHEET 3

SEE DETAIL J
SHEET 4

SEE DETAIL B
SHEET 2

SEE DETAIL H
SHEET 4

SEE DETAIL A
SHEET 2

SEE DETAIL G
SHEET 3

SEE DETAIL C
SHEET 2

SEE DETAIL D
SHEET 2

SEE DETAIL E
SHEET 3

72 75 74 70 73 71 69 55 24 67 23 91 68

15A-4-1-(125-1)

The F-15's fuselage is built in three sections, primarily for ease of manufacturing. The three sections are all-metal, semi-monocoque structures, constructed primarily of aluminum with some titanium in high-stress and high-heat areas. The center fuselage is the primary structural piece in the F-15, and provides the main attachment point for the wings, and the hard point for the speed brake actuator. It also includes the tunnels to duct air from the air intakes to the engines. The center fuselage contains the mechanical parts of the M61 cannon, the 20MM

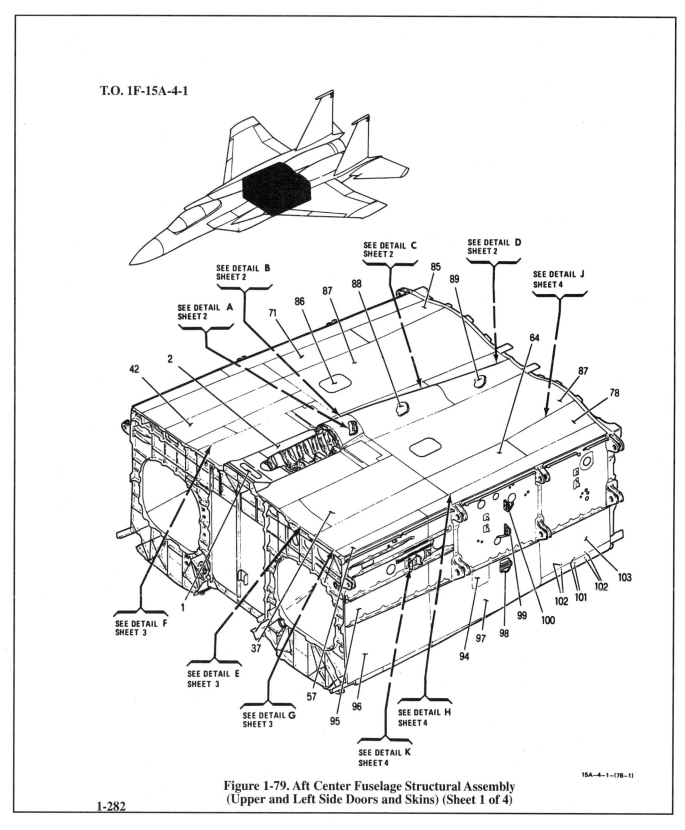

Figure 1-79. Aft Center Fuselage Structural Assembly
(Upper and Left Side Doors and Skins) (Sheet 1 of 4)

15A–4–1–(7B–1)

1-282

ammunition drum, and fuel cells. A truss structure allows the wing loads to be carried around the engine air ducts, permitting a lower weight, smaller cross-section configuration. The wing torque box is a multi-cell, three-spar, structure utilizing multi-stiffened skins to carry the bending loads into the fuselage through three pairs of pinned lugs. (U.S. Air Force)

STRIKE 5 EAGLE

Originally, the F-15 had been conceived as a multi-role aircraft, but the fighter role become paramount, and by 1975 the air-to-ground role had been largely forgotten. However, during the late 1970s, McDonnell Douglas and Hughes Aircraft collaborated in a privately-funded study of the feasibility of adapting the basic F-15 airframe to the air-to-ground role.

As part of project Strike Eagle, McDonnell Douglas converted the second TF-15A (71-0291) into a dedicated interdiction aircraft that first flew on 8 July 1980. Limited funding was provided by the Air Force under the Advanced Fighter Capability Demonstrator (AFCD) program and the Strike Eagle demonstrator was displayed at the 1980 Farnborough air show in the hope of attracting customers. This aircraft was later equipped with a Pave Tack laser designator pod (as used on some F-4Es and F-111Fs) enabling it to deliver "smart" laser-guided bombs without the assistance of a separate designator aircraft.

In the meantime, the Air Force had begun studying concepts for an Enhanced Tactical Fighter (ETF) that would replace the General Dynamics F-111. In the interest of cost, the Air Force decided to explore conversions of existing aircraft such as the F-15 or F-16 that could meet the ETF requirement rather than to try and develop an entirely new aircraft. The Panavia Tornado was initially considered, but it was eliminated from consideration early because of its short range and its obvious political disadvantage of not being made in the United States.

The ETF studies (later renamed Dual-Role Fighter) led to a competition between the Strike Eagle and the cranked arrow-wing F-16XL Scamp prototypes. McDonnell Douglas began flight testing the new systems for the F-15E on an F-15B (77-0166), F-15C (78-0468), and the Strike Eagle demonstrator (71-0291) in November 1982. The demonstration program was completed on 30 April 1983 after more than 200 flights which included a take-off by 71-0291 weighing more than 75,000 pounds. On this occasion the aircraft was equipped with two conformal fuel tanks, three 610 gallon external tanks, and eight 500 pound Mk 82 bombs.

The Air Force announced on 24 February 1984 that it had selected the F-15E for continued development, primarily because of its lower development costs, projected to be $270 million versus $470 million for the F-16XL. It was also believed the F-15E had more future growth potential, and was less susceptible to combat damage due to its twin engine configuration. Detailed design work began in April 1984 under a $359.4 million fixed-price contract.

Some 30 percent of the F-15's structure was redesigned to create the F-15E, and the airframe is expected to have a 16,000 flight hour fatigue life. All previous two-seaters had not carried the ALQ-135 ECM system since on single-seaters this is normally located where the second seat goes. This system was deemed essential to

The General Electric F110 engine has never been used operationally in the F-15, although all F-15Es are capable of using it. Modern jet engines are becoming remarkably "clean" with little of the extensive piping and tubing seen on earlier generations of engines. (Dennis R. Jenkins)

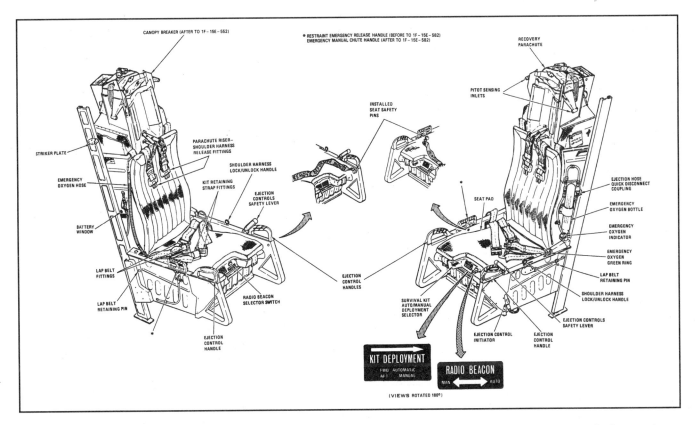

CANOPY BREAKER (AFTER TO 1F–15E–552)

* RESTRAINT EMERGENCY RELEASE HANDLE (BEFORE TO 1F–15E–582)
EMERGENCY MANUAL CHUTE HANDLE (AFTER TO 1F–15E–582)

RECOVERY PARACHUTE

PITOT SENSING INLETS

INSTALLED SEAT SAFETY PINS

PARACHUTE RISER–SHOULDER HARNESS RELEASE FITTINGS

STRIKER PLATE

SHOULDER HARNESS LOCK/UNLOCK HANDLE

EMERGENCY OXYGEN HOSE

KIT RETAINING STRAP FITTINGS

EJECTION CONTROLS SAFETY LEVER

EJECTION HOSE QUICK DISCONNECT COUPLING

EMERGENCY OXYGEN BOTTLE

EMERGENCY OXYGEN INDICATOR

EMERGENCY OXYGEN GREEN RING

BATTERY WINDOW

SEAT PAD

LAP BELT RETAINING PIN

LAP BELT FITTINGS

SHOULDER HARNESS LOCK/UNLOCK HANDLE

RADIO BEACON SELECTOR SWITCH

EJECTION CONTROL HANDLES

LAP BELT RETAINING PIN

SURVIVAL KIT AUTO/MANUAL DEPLOYMENT SELECTOR

EJECTION CONTROLS SAFETY LEVER

EJECTION CONTROL HANDLE

EJECTION CONTROL INITIATOR

EJECTION CONTROL HANDLE

KIT DEPLOYMENT
FWD   AUTOMATIC
AFT   MANUAL

RADIO BEACON
MAN ←→ AUTO

(VIEWS ROTATED 180°)

The ejection seat in the F-15 provides escape from zero knots at zero altitude throughout the F-15's flight envelope. For years the US believed it provided the best ejection seats possible for its pilots but the break-up of the Soviet Union has allowed evaluation of Russian ejection seats that have generally been found to be superior to US seats in every regard. This was well illustrated by a spectacular crash of a MiG-29 at the Paris air show when the pilot managed to eject even as his aircraft's nose was impacting the ground in a near vertical dive. (U.S. Air Force)

the Strike Eagle's strike interdiction mission. To accommodate the ALQ-135 system, the forward avionics bays were completely redesigned, the internal fuel capacity reduced 51 gallons to 2,019 gallons by redesigning the forward fuel tank, and the 20MM ammunition capacity cut in half to 450 rounds.

A complete redesign of the entire aft fuselage provided a common engine bay (officially called the "F110 Compatible Fuselage") that enables the F-15E to be powered by either the P&W F100 or the General Electric F110. The engine bay structure consists of large titanium sections manufactured with superplastic forming and diffu-

Without knowing it, the public relations photographer took a picture of the future. In February 1976, the second TF-15A (71-0291) posed on the dry lake at Edwards with a load of bombs. Four years later, this same aircraft would take to the air as the Strike Eagle demonstrator, with a dedicated strike-interdiction mission. The engine inlets are in their full-down position. (McDonnell Douglas)

The first true production F-15E (86-0186) was assigned to the 405th Tactical Training Wing at Luke AFB. In this photo, it was painted as the Wing commander's aircraft, and carried a colored stripe for each squadron assigned to the wing. Noteworthy is the slightly different configuration of the rear formation light strip on the aft fuselage, typical of all F-15Es, most MSIP-II F-15C/Ds, and some MSIP F-15A/Bs. The reason for the change is not readily apparent. (Mick Roth)

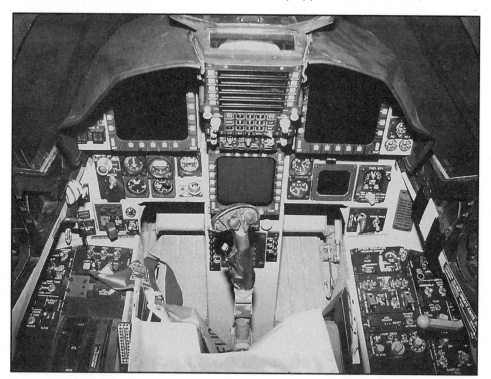

The front cockpit of the F-15E shows the transition the military is making to multi-purpose displays instead of dedicated instruments. This has greatly eased the burden of integrating new weapons and sensor systems into the aircraft. Conventional engine and flight instruments are used as backups in case of a catastrophic failure of the electronic system. (Dennis R. Jenkins)

sion bonding processes, and will permit installation of future growth versions of the engines. The F-15E also incorporates digital electronic engine controls, foam filled fuel tanks for greater survivability, higher rated electric generators, an improved environmental control system, strengthened landing gear, and larger wheels and tires.

Construction of three F-15Es began in July 1985, and the first (86-0183) made its initial flight on 11 December 1986 piloted by McDonnell Douglas test pilot Gary Jennings. The flight lasted 75 minutes and reached Mach 0.9 and 40,000 feet. This aircraft had the redesigned forward fuselage and carried the full complement of F-15E avionics and displays, but did not have the new aft fuselage or common engine bay. The second and third aircraft are generally considered to be pre-production aircraft, with 86-0184 becoming the first to receive the common engine bay, and 86-0185 being the first aircraft to incorporate all production features. Five additional aircraft were ordered in FY86, and the first production F-15E (86-0186), powered by a pair of F100-PW-220 engines, was delivered to the 33rd TFW at Eglin AFB in August 1986.

The rear cockpit of the F-15E has been upgraded with four multi-purpose CRT displays for radar, weapons selection and monitoring of

An unusual configuration for the F-15E—AIM-7s mounted on type-4 CFTs. It is more common to see bombs mounted on the CFTs, relying on AIM-9s carried on the wing pylons for self-defense. LANTIRN pods are mounted beneath the air intakes. Unusual is the marking inside the nose wheel door—normally the last three or four numbers of the aircraft serial number is painted here for the benefit of ground crews. This aircraft carries "E001" to signify that it is the first F-15E (86-0183). (Dennis R. Jenkins)

enemy tracking systems and also contains two hand controllers for the radar and LANTIRN units. The aft cockpit retains the flight control stick and essential flight instrumentation. A synthetic aperture radar feature was added to the APG-70 to provide almost photographic quality imagery in all weather. Front cockpit modifications include redesigned "up-front" controls, a wide field of vision HUD, and three CRTs that provide multi-purpose displays of navigation, weapons delivery and systems operations, including moving map displays, weapons options, precision radar mapping and terrain following. A digital, triple-redundant Lear Siegler Astronautics flight control system has been

The control stick of the F-15E is nearly as busy as the throttle. Many of the switches have different actions when the aircraft is on the ground and in the air. For example, the paddle switch actuated by the little finger disengages the nose wheel steering when on the ground, but disengages the autopilot when in the air. Alternately, the switch can also override the terrain following radar and disengages the built-in test for the automatic flight control system. (U.S. Air Force)

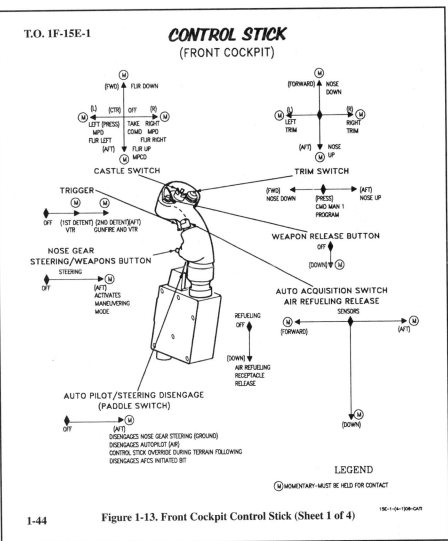

Figure 1-13. Front Cockpit Control Stick (Sheet 1 of 4)

One of the more popular weapons during the Gulf War was the AGM-65 Maverick missile. The F-15E was capable of carrying up to six Mavericks (three under each wing). Here an F-15E (88-0707) carries a single Maverick training missile under its wing while at Nellis AFB. The pod directly above the maverick is an ASQ-T11 air combat maneuvering instrumentation pod, which mounts in the same location as a Sidewinder missile. (Craig Kaston via the Mick Roth Collection)

A standard USAF bomb truck is used by most Air Force units to carry bombs from their storage areas to the flight line. These bombs will be loaded aboard an F-15E (90-0233) from the 90th Fighter Squadron (21st FW) at Nellis AFB. This unit is normally based at Elmendorf AFB, Alaska. (David F. Brown via the Mick Roth Collection)

installed to permit coupled automatic terrain following.

A key element of the F-15E's weapons delivery system is the Lockheed Martin LANTIRN (Low-Altitude Navigation and Targeting Infra-Red for Night) system, which consists of a pod carried underneath each air intake. The AAQ-13 navigation pod is carried on the starboard station and contains a FLIR camera which displays a high-quality video image of the oncoming terrain on the pilot's heads-up display, enabling high-speed low-level flights to be made at night under clear weather conditions.

The navigation pod also carries a Ku-Band terrain-following radar which is effective in bad weather. The pilot can manually respond to cues from the system or can couple the system to the flight controls for "hands-off" automatic terrain-following flight at altitudes as low as 200 feet. The AAQ-14 targeting pod is carried on the port station and contains a missile boresight correlator and a laser designator. The boresight correlator is used to guide the Maverick air-to-surface missile and the laser designator is used for weapons such as laser guided bombs that home in on reflected laser light.

THROTTLE QUADRANT
(FRONT)

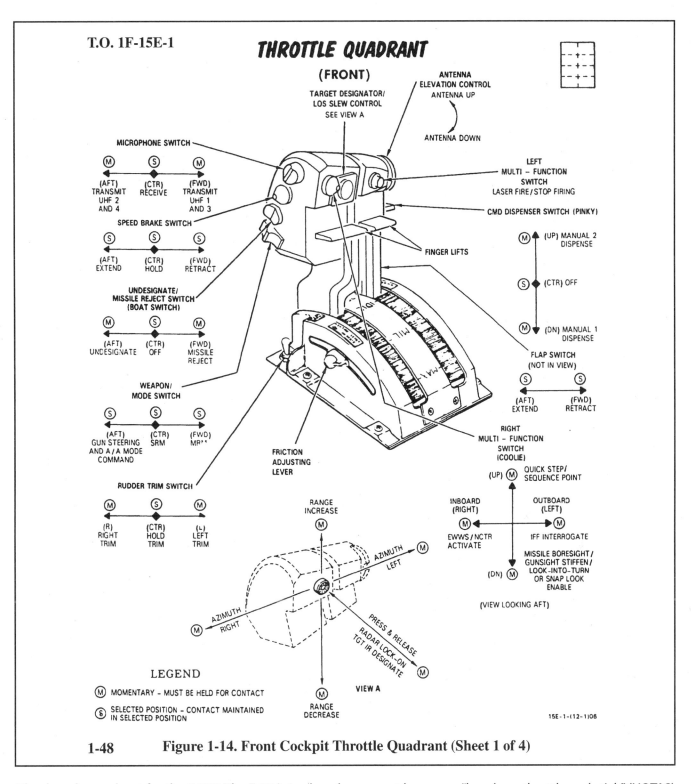

Figure 1-14. Front Cockpit Throttle Quadrant (Sheet 1 of 4)

1-48

The throttle quadrant for the F-15E. The F-15 introduced a concept known as "hands on throttle and stick" (HOTAS) that permitted the pilot to actuate most of the important switches without removing his hands from the throttle and control stick during air combat. Although this has improved things dramatically for the pilot, it has created extremely complicated controls on the throttle. For example, the pilot's thumb has four different switches to operate on the side of the throttle, including keying the microphone, positioning the speed brake, undesignating a target, and switching weapons mode (guns, short-range missiles, medium-range missiles). All of his other fingers are equally as busy. This illustration shows an odd perspective, and the front of the aircraft is oriented towards the right-lower corner of the throttle quadrant. (U.S. Air Force)

McDONNELL DOUGLAS
F-15 EAGLE

The F-15E's 23,500 pound air-to-ground weapons load is carried on six tangential stubs on the corner of each type-4 conformal fuel tank. The F-15E also retains the full air-to-air capability of other Eagles, and can carry AIM-7 or AIM-120 missiles on the stub pylons on the CFTs, in addition to AIM-9 or AIM-120 missiles on the wing pylons.

F-15Es (87-0202) can carry a wide variety of air-to-ground ordnance, including the cluster bombs shown here, on the conformal fuel tanks. The CFTs cover part of the articulating inlet, although it does not affect its operation. Slightly darker patches just above and forward of the pitot tube are the forward ALQ-128 antennas. As usual, the radome paint does not match. (Ben Knowles via the Mick Roth Collection)

External identifying features of the F-15E include bulged main gear doors to accommodate the larger wheel/tire assemblies, a small bulge on the underside of the fuselage under the 20MM ammunition drum, two ALQ-135B radomes on the aft fuselage booms, a completely redesigned tail hook with no doors, and a redesigned fairing between the engine

This F-15E (88-1690) from the 4th TFW shows the two different ALQ-135 antennas that have begun appearing on the Eagle. The left (near) boom uses the normal round antenna that has been seen for years on F-15Cs and F-15Es, while the right (far) boom shows the new "square" antenna. All F-15Es are equipped with one of each antenna in the configuration shown here. F-15Cs only have an antenna on the right boom, and both styles have been observed. The square antenna is normally seen an aircraft equipped with the ALQ 135B band-3 antennas on the nose, so it is assumed to be related to that recent modification. (Dennis R. Jenkins)

exhaust nozzles. Of course, the fact that all F-15Es have been painted very dark gray instead of the normal two-tone Compass Ghost also helps identify them.

A total of 48 F-15Es were ordered in FY87, although six were subsequently cancelled when insufficient funds were authorized by Congress. The next year brought orders for 42 more. Thirty-six were ordered in FY89, but then cancelled when funds were not made available. However, later in the year funding was restored, and the 36 aircraft were reinstated, although with different serial numbers. Unfortunately, growing budget pressures resulted in a concerted effort to cancel procurement of the F-15E during the early 1990s. The aircraft's performance during Operation Desert Storm brought temporary relief when Congress allowed attrition aircraft to be procured, and a limited number of new aircraft have

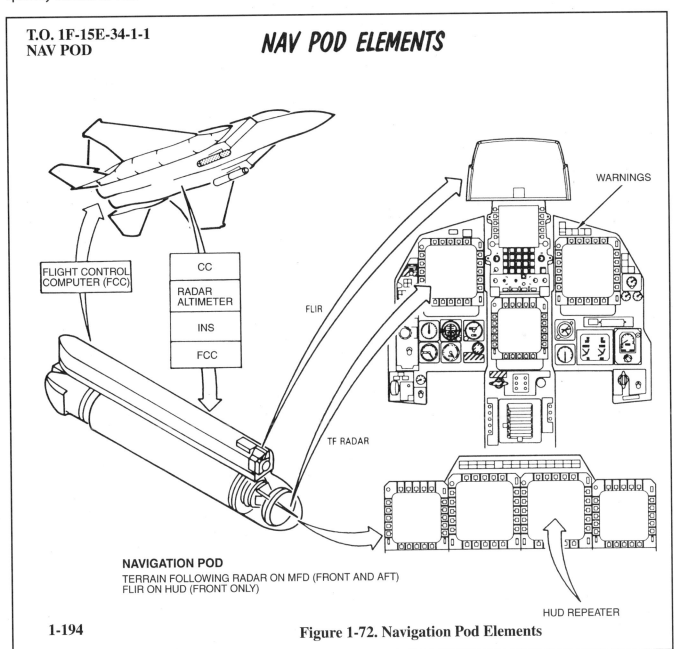

T.O. 1F-15E-34-1-1
NAV POD

NAV POD ELEMENTS

WARNINGS

FLIGHT CONTROL COMPUTER (FCC)

CC

RADAR ALTIMETER

INS

FCC

FLIR

TF RADAR

NAVIGATION POD
TERRAIN FOLLOWING RADAR ON MFD (FRONT AND AFT)
FLIR ON HUD (FRONT ONLY)

HUD REPEATER

1-194

Figure 1-72. Navigation Pod Elements

The F-15E introduced a new cockpit based on multi-function CRTs instead of conventional flight instruments. This permits the display of terrain following radar images from the LANTIRN navigation pod. The F-15E front cockpit also introduced a new wide-angle field-of-view heads up display (HUD) that can also display infrared images from the LANTIRN pod. The "guy in back" can display the HUD image on one of his multi-function displays. (U.S. Air Force)

been ordered each year throughout the 1990s. The 1997 defense spending authorization contains $275 million for six additional F-15Es, or roughly $46 million per copy, including spares and support. (This compares to $155 million for six F-16Cs in the 1997 budget, or roughly $26 million each). The fact that Israeli and Saudi aircraft are built on the same assembly lines means that the USAF can continue to buy F-15Es at an uneconomical rate for the foreseeable future. McDonnell Douglas projects that the USAF will order six additional F-15Es in FY98, with a need for up to 40 more in future years.

Following completion of operational test and evaluation at Edwards and weapons separation tests at Eglin, production F-15Es were delivered to the 461st TFTS of the 405th TTW at Luke AFB in July 1988. The first operational F-15E unit was the 336th TFS of the 4th TFW, stationed at Seymour Johnson AFB in North Carolina, which achieved initial IOC in October 1989. In June 1990, the F-15E participated for the first time in the Long Rifle gunnery competition held at Davis-Monthan AFB, and scored first and second place.

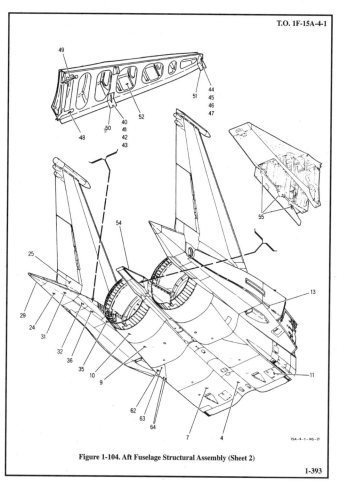

Figure 1-104. Aft Fuselage Structural Assembly (Sheet 2)

1-393

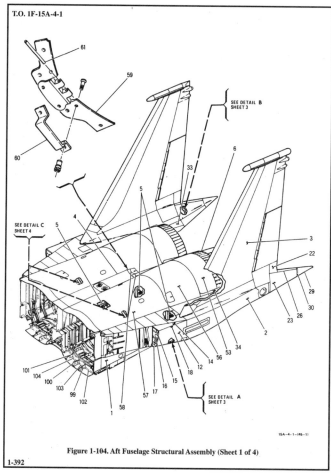

Figure 1-104. Aft Fuselage Structural Assembly (Sheet 1 of 4)

1-392

To increase aft fuselage structural efficiency, engine removal/installation is accomplished from the rear of the aircraft, with the engines sliding on rails contained on each side of each engine bay. The engines are separated by a titanium web keel which supports the arresting hook. The keel also protects the second engine from damage caused by a catastrophic failure of the first, enhancing survivability. A fire extinguishing system is fitted in both engine bays, a first for an American fighter. The aft fuselage also provides the attachment points for the horizontal and vertical stabilizers. There were initially some problems with stress cracking and corrosion around the attachments for the vertical stabilizer, but these were largely taken care of with slightly revised drains and painting techniques. The horizontal stabilizers attach by means of a single rod through the hole shown between #2 and #23. The aft fuselage also contains the arresting hook, and the fairing shown containing the three #55 callouts was deleted from the F-15E, and has been removed from many earlier F-15s. The vertical and horizontal stabilizers are identical from side to side, and can be interchanged. (U.S. Air Force)

MK-82 LDGP, SNAKEYE 1 LOW DRAG BOMBS
DIVE RELEASE
5.0G TURNING MANEUVER
TARGET DENSITY ALTITUDE – 5000 FEET

RELEASE		SAFE ESCAPE/SAFE SEPARATION						
		SINGLE		RIPPLE – 6 BOMBS				
DIVE ANGLE	TAS	MINIMUM		30 MSEC		75 FEET		150 FEET
		REL ALT	TIME OF FALL	MIN REL ALT	IMPACT SPACING	MIN REL ALT	INTV SET	MIN REL ALT	INTV SET
DEG	KNOTS	FEET	SEC	FEET	FEET	FEET	MSEC	FEET	MSEC
0	450	520	5.13	560	23	610	99	700	197
	500	480	4.90	510	25	560	89	640	178
	550	420	4.55	450	28	490	81	560	162
	600	390	4.38	420	30	440	74	500	148
	650	380	4.33	410	32	430	70	480	140
5	450	770	4.77	820	17	930	133	1090	259
	500	750	4.55	800	18	900	124	1040	243
	550	710	4.25	760	19	850	119	1000	230
	600	690	4.05	740	19	810	114	940	220
	650	700	4.00	740	20	820	109	930	212
10	450	1070	4.74	1130	13	1330	167	1570	323
	500	1080	4.56	1140	14	1330	159	1550	309
	550	1040	4.23	1110	14	1300	155	1540	298
	600	1050	4.09	1100	14	1260	152	1470	294
	650	1070	4.01	1130	15	1280	147	1470	285
15	450	1380	4.77	1450	11	1730	199	2060	379
	500	1410	4.58	1480	11	1760	195	2090	370
	550	1390	4.29	1470	11	1770	193	2130	363
	600	1410	4.13	1480	11	1750	192	2080	362
	650	1460	4.08	1530	11	1760	188	2040	360
20	450	1680	4.78	1760	9	2170	230	2590	433
	500	1720	4.57	1810	9	2220	228	2660	428
	550	1730	4.32	1830	9	2280	226	2720	425
	600	1770	4.18	1850	9	2280	229	2740	428
	650	1830	4.11	1920	9	2300	227	2680	433

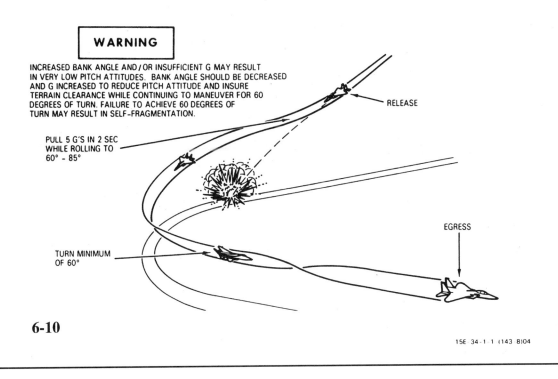

WARNING

INCREASED BANK ANGLE AND / OR INSUFFICIENT G MAY RESULT IN VERY LOW PITCH ATTITUDES. BANK ANGLE SHOULD BE DECREASED AND G INCREASED TO REDUCE PITCH ATTITUDE AND INSURE TERRAIN CLEARANCE WHILE CONTINUING TO MANEUVER FOR 60 DEGREES OF TURN. FAILURE TO ACHIEVE 60 DEGREES OF TURN MAY RESULT IN SELF-FRAGMENTATION.

RELEASE

PULL 5 G'S IN 2 SEC WHILE ROLLING TO 60° - 85°

TURN MINIMUM OF 60°

EGRESS

6-10

15E-34-1-1 (143-8)04

The F-15E conventional weapons manual has many pages dedicated to charts and diagrams such as this one that show pilots how to effectively use the weapons they carry. The flight profiles generally involve a significant amount of maneuvering (such as the 5g 60° roll immediately after weapons release shown here), and numerous warnings about how not to be caught in the blast of the weapons just dropped. The general air-to-ground weapons release speed is between 450 and 650 knots at dive angles between 5 and 20 degrees. (U.S. Air Force)

FOREIGN EAGLES

Iran was the first foreign country to take an interest in the F-15 during July 1973 when the Shah personally examined both the F-14 and the F-15 at Andrews AFB. Iran needed an aircraft capable of shooting down the MiG-25, and thus chose the Phoenix equipped F-14, since the F-15 had not yet demonstrated this capability. Also, the F-14 was available for earlier delivery than the F-15. As late as 1975, McDonnell Douglas foresaw a possibility of selling 200 F-15s to Germany, 170 to Great Britain, 100 to Japan, 53 to Iran, 50 to Australia, and 50 to Canada. Germany had evaluated the aircraft in March 1975, Canada in June and then again in September 1975, and

Great Britain during October 1975. In fact, a sale to France seemed so certain that the second TF-15A (71-0291) spent a week painted in French Air Force markings in April 1976 while giving demonstrations to French pilots at Edwards. However, primarily due to its high cost, only three countries, Israel, Japan, and Saudi Arabia, have actually purchased the aircraft to date. For the most part exported Eagles look and fly like their American counterparts. In every case the ability to carry and deliver the B61 "special" (nuclear) store has been deleted, and usually the more classified pieces of electronic countermeasures have not been included. This is evidenced by the lack of ECM

antennas on top of the left vertical stabilizer, on the aft fuselage booms, and under the forward fuselage on all export Eagles, including the F-15I/S variants.

F-15 IN ISRAEL

Israel had long been interested in the F-15 Eagle for the *Tsvah Haganah le Israel-Heyl Ha'Avir* (Israel Defense Force/Air Force, or IDF/AF) and four Israeli pilots and one radar operator flew the first TF-15A (71-0290) at Edwards in September 1974. This was Israel's first formal evaluation of the F-15, and the aircraft was pitted against a slatted F-4E during air combat maneuvers. The F-15 won, handily.

The French were interested in the FAST Pack concept, and several demonstration flights were flown with the CFTs in place on the fuselage sides of T2 (71-0291). French roundels were on the upper and lower surface of both wings. The French markings were applied in St. Louis, and the aircraft was then flown to Edwards for the demonstration. The markings were removed at Edwards, and for several weeks the aircraft was flown with no national insignia at all. Note the mounting of the forward Sparrow missile. (Dennis R. Jenkins)

Four Category II test F-15As (72-0116/0118 and 72-0120) were refurbished under the FMS Peace Fox I program and delivered to Israel on 11 December 1976. Although refurbished, these were not brought up to production standards prior to delivery, and retained the small speed brake characteristic of the test aircraft.

Israel subsequently purchased an additional 19 F-15As (76-1505/1523), and two F-15Bs (76-

1524/1525) under Peace Fox II. In 1982, a single USAF F-15A (76-0120) was transferred to Israel as a replacement for an F-15 that was lost due to a bird strike. Peace Fox III provided 18 F-15Cs (80-0122/0130 and 83-0054/0062) and eight F-15Ds (80-0131/0136 and 83-0063/0064) beginning in mid-1982. The Israeli's have named their F-15A/Bs *Baz* (Eagle), and their F-15C/Ds *Akef* (Buzzard).

The Israeli aircraft differ from the USAF F-15s in having ARC-109 radios in place of the ARC-164, and, like other non-USAF aircraft, the Israeli Eagles do not have an ALQ-128 pod on top of the left vertical stabilizer. All Israeli aircraft use the IC-7 ejection system instead of the ACES II used by later USAF F-15C/Ds. Israeli aircraft are capable of carrying an indigenously produced AL/L-8202 ECM pod in addition to US-supplied ALQ-119 and ALQ-131 pods. All *Heyl Ha'Avir* F-15s, including the four refurbished test aircraft, are capable of carrying conformal fuel tanks, which are manufactured locally by Israeli Aircraft Industries. In addition to the normal AIM-9s, Israeli F-15s can also carry the Israeli-built Shafrir and Python infrared homing missiles.

Israel purchased five additional F-15D aircraft (90-0275/0279) in early 1989 under Peace Fox IV for use as long-range strike aircraft. No details have been released, but it is believed that these aircraft utilized the basic F-15E airframe since the original F-15C/D airframe was not in production at the time.

No. 133 Squadron of the IDF/AF was formed specifically to operate the F-15A/B, with No. 106 Squadron operating the F-15C/D.

Both squadrons are based at Tel Nof. There have also been reports the Nos. 144 and 149(R) Squadrons at Hatzor operate several F-15s in specialized (probably Wild Weasel/SEAD) roles. Israel jealously guards its security, and few other squadron details are available.

The IDF/AF has fitted home-built self-defense systems to their F-15s, including chaff and flare dispensers. In addition, most of the older F-15A/Bs have had their computer systems and avionics upgraded to F-15C/D standards utilizing Israeli hardware. It has been reported that Israel is to receive a batch of early F-15As from the USAF that were not scheduled for the MSIP and would otherwise be scrapped or placed in storage. These deliveries are supposedly taking place as a *quid pro quo* for Israel's decision not to retaliate against Iraqi Scud launches during the Gulf War, but these had not been delivered by late-1996, making it unlikely they ever will be.

F-15I

On 27 January 1994 the Israeli government announced the intention to purchase the F-15I, a version of the F-15E designed specifically

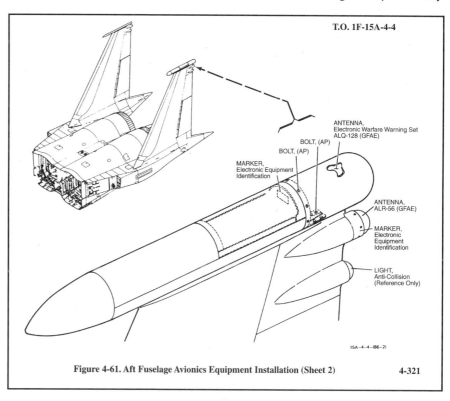

Figure 4-61. Aft Fuselage Avionics Equipment Installation (Sheet 2)   4-321

The left vertical stabilizer has a pod that contains the rear-looking antenna for the Magnavox ALQ-128 electronic warfare warning system (EWWS). Additional antennas are located behind panels on each side of the forward fuselage. The actual functions and capabilities of this system are so classified that unclassified documentation, which normally will contain at least a short description of a classified system, says nothing other than referring the reader to a classified supplement. This pod is absent from all foreign F-15s except for the 24 ex-USAF F-15C/Ds sent to Saudi Arabia during the Gulf War. In those aircraft the ALQ-128 system was removed, but the pod remains. (U.S. Air Force)

A F-15DJ (JASDF 42-8060, USAF 81-0071) touches down. The Japanese F-15s are externally similar to the USAF aircraft except for the lack of ECM antennas on the top of the left vertical stabilizer and under the forward fuselage. The size of the speed brake shows up well in this view. Japanese aircraft carry national insignia on the top and bottom of both wings, in addition to on each side of the forward fuselage. (Toshiki Kudo)

for Israel. A $2.4 billion contract (Peace Fox V) was signed on 12 May 1994 between the governments of the United States and Israel authorizing McDonnell Douglas to build 21 F-15Is for the IDF/AF to be delivered at a rate of one per month beginning in early 1997. On 1 December 1995 Lockheed Martin received an FMS contract worth $74.2 million to build 23 LANTIRN navigation pods for Israel's F-15I. The No. 69 Squadron at Hetzerim will trade their F-4Es for F-15Is to become the first operational squadron to operate the type. In early 1996 Israel exercised an option for an additional four F-15Is under Peace Fox VI. The F-15I is named *Ra'am* (Thunder) in Israeli service.

F-15J/DJ in Japan

During June-July 1975, Japanese pilots evaluated the F-15 at Edwards AFB, and in December 1977 it was announced that the F-15 had been selected to replace the Lockheed F-104J Starfighters

serving with the *Nihon Koku Jietai* (Japanese Air Self Defense Force, or JASDF). Single-seat Japanese Eagles are designated F-15J, with the two-seat version being F-15DJ.

A license was acquired from McDonnell Douglas and the US government for a group led by Mitsubishi to manufacture the F-15 in Japan. Plans called for the first two F-15Js and 12 F-15DJs to be manufactured by McDonnell Douglas in St. Louis under project Peace Eagle with the remainder manufactured in Japan by Mitsubishi at its plant in Komaki. A similar arrangement had been used for Japanese manufacture of the F-4 Phantom.

The Japanese F-15s are substantially similar to early production F-15C/Ds, with the primary differences being the substitution of Japanese-built electronic countermeasures systems. Among the indigenous equipment fitted to the F-15J/DJ is the J/ALQ-8 ECM suite and the XJ/APQ-1 radar warning system. JASDF Eagles were initially powered by F100-PW-100 turbofans, but beginning in 1991, these were replaced by F100-PW-220s, and by improved -220E engines in 1996.

One of the St. Louis-built F-15DJs (JASDF 12-8052, USAF 79-0283) returns to base. There is remarkably little detail inside the speed brake well or the underside of the speed brake itself on later F-15s. The first 30 operational USAF aircraft had extensive framing and bracing on the underside of the speed brake. The lack of ALQ-128/135 antennas on the rear fuselage booms and vertical stabilizer of JASDF aircraft is evident. (Toshiki Kudo)

F-15 DIMENSION DATA

	F-15 A	F-15 B	F-15 C/J	F-15 D/DJ	F-15 E/I/S/U	F-15 K/U(Plus)
WING SPAN (FT)	42.81	42.81	42.81	42.81	42.81	42.81
LENGTH (FT)	63.75	63.75	63.75	63.75	63.75	63.75
HEIGHT (FT)	18.46	18.46	18.46	18.46	18.46	18.46
TAILPLANE SPAN (FT)	28.25	28.25	28.25	28.25	28.25	28.25
WHEEL TRACK (FT)	9.00	9.00	9.00	9.00	9.00	9.00
WHEEL BASE (FT)	17.79	17.79	17.79	17.79	17.79	17.79
WING AREA, GROSS (SQ FT)	608.00	608.00	608.00	608.00	608.00	743.00
AILERON AREA, TOTAL (SQ FT)	26.48	26.48	26.48	26.48	26.48	26.48
FLAP AREA, TOTAL (SQ FT)	35.84	35.84	35.84	35.84	35.84	35.84
FIN AREA, TOTAL (SQ FT)	105.28	105.28	105.28	105.28	105.28	105.28
RUDDER AREA, TOTAL (SQ FT)	19.94	19.94	19.94	19.94	19.94	19.94
TAILPLANES, TOTAL (SQ FT)	111.36	111.36	111.36	111.36	111.36	111.36
EMPTY WEIGHT (LBS)	26,500	27,300	28,200	28,800	31,700	36,000
MAX T-O WEIGHT (LBS)	56,000	56,000	68,470	68,470	84,000	90,000
COMBAT WEIGHT (LBS)	41,000	41,000	44,000	44,000	52,600	58,000
INTERNAL FUEL (GALS)	1,759	1,759	2,070	2,070	2,019	2,727
(F-15A/B-10 AND SUBS)	1,759	1,759	—	—	—	—

The first two F-15Js (USAF 79-0280/0281, JASDF 02-8801/8802) were built in St. Louis, with the first one making its initial flight on 4 June 1980. The next eight (JASDF 12-8803, 22-8804/8810) were assembled by Mitsubishi from knock-down kits supplied by McDonnell Douglas, and the first Japanese-assembled F-15J (12-8803) flew at Komaki on 26 August 1981. The JASDF has a complicated six-digit serial system with the first digit corresponding to the last digit in the procurement year (0 = 1980, 1 = 1981, etc.), the second the basic class of aircraft (2 = multi-engine), the third the basic role (8 = all-weather fighter), and the last three digits the individual aircraft number in sequence. In 1990, the unit cost of the F-15J was estimated at US$55.2 million representing a significant premium of the cost of USAF F-15Cs (or even F-15Es). As of 1996, the F-15J/DJ continues in low-rate production, with procurements expected to continue through 2000.

The F-15J's service evaluation was carried out by the *Koku Jikkendan* (Air Proving Wing) at Gifu AB on Honshu. The first operational squadron was 202 *Hikotai* (Squadron) of 5 *Kokudan* (Air Wing), which began receiving Eagles in 1981, replacing F-104J Starfighters. In 1986/87, Eagles began to replace

For years the Israeli Air Force would not release photos of its aircraft, and is still sensitive about it. Here, a pair of IDF/AF F-15As is shown on their delivery flight from the United States to Israel. Except for the lack of ALQ-128/135 antennas, the IDF/AF aircraft are externally identical to their USAF counterparts. However, like almost all IDF/AF aircraft, they have been extensively modified in Israel, and have capabilities that in some cases exceed those of USAF models. (Dennis R. Jenkins Collection)

the F-4EJ in JASDF service, the first unit to convert being 303 Hikotai at Komatsu. In addition, six F-15DJs are assigned to the *Hiko Kyodotai*, an aggressor squadron based at Nyutabaru. Problems with the Mitsubishi T-2's low power and excessively-high accident rate led to a decision to adopt the F-15DJ for the aggressor squadron.

F-15 IN SAUDI ARABIA

The *Al Quwwat al Jawwiya as Saudiya* (Royal Saudi Air Force, or RSAF) obtained 46 F-15Cs (80-0062/0106 and 81-0002) and 16 F-15Ds (80-0107/0121 and 81-0003) under the FMS Peace Sun program to replace their aging BAC Lightnings. The original Saudi order was for 47 F-15Cs and 15 F-15Ds, but on the production line a USAF F-15D (81-0066) was swapped for an RSAF F-15C (81-0003) which became USAF F-15C 81-0056, with the new Saudi two-seater carrying the same serial number as the single-seater it replaced (81-0003). The Saudi aircraft are

externally identical to USAF versions except for the lack of an ALQ-128 pod on the top of the left vertical stabilizer and the lack of ALQ-135 antennas on the fuselage booms and under the forward fuselage.

The delivery of F-15s to Saudi Arabia has always been controversial, with Israel and its supporters in

the US Congress being unhappy about such an advanced warplane being in the hands of a potential adversary. Although the US Congress eventually did approve the sale, a limit was imposed in 1980 which restricted Saudi Arabia to having no more than 60 Eagles in the country at any one time. Consequently the last two F-15Cs were retained by McDonnell Douglas as attrition aircraft. There were also restrictions placed on the delivery of the associated conformal fuel tanks to Saudi Arabia, which would have brought Israel within range. It should be noted however, that all Saudi Eagles are CFT-capable, and that at least a limited number of CFTs were transferred to the RSAF during the Gulf war.

Some of the early RSAF F-15s, wearing USAF markings, were used at Luke AFB to train a cadre of Saudi air and ground crews. The first F-15C/Ds arrived in Saudi Arabia on 11 August 1981, and have since been supplied to No. 5 Squadron at King Fahad AFB in Taif, No. 6 at King Khaled AFB in Khamis

The first Royal Saudi Air Force F-15D (80-0107) was initially used at Luke AFB as a trainer for Saudi pilots, complete with USAF markings. The aircraft is readily identifiable by its lack of an ALQ-128 antenna on the left vertical stabilizer. Otherwise, it was identical to the USAF F-15Ds on the flight line. The aircraft was later ferried to Saudi Arabia, although some Saudi pilots still train at Luke using USAF F-15s. (Dennis R. Jenkins)

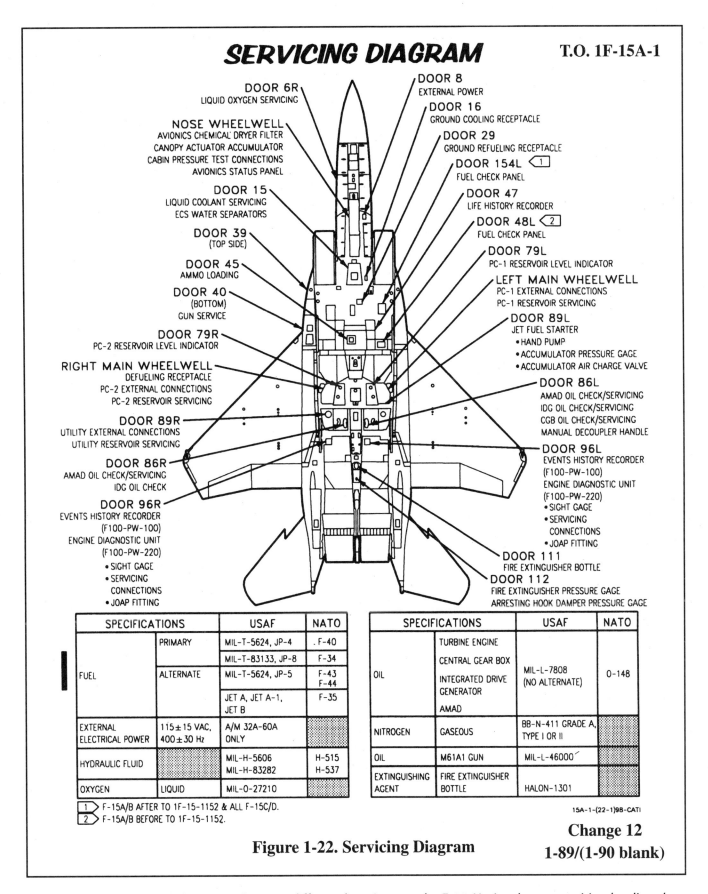

SERVICING DIAGRAM T.O. 1F-15A-1

DOOR 6R
LIQUID OXYGEN SERVICING

DOOR 8
EXTERNAL POWER

DOOR 16
GROUND COOLING RECEPTACLE

NOSE WHEELWELL
AVIONICS CHEMICAL DRYER FILTER
CANOPY ACTUATOR ACCUMULATOR
CABIN PRESSURE TEST CONNECTIONS
AVIONICS STATUS PANEL

DOOR 29
GROUND REFUELING RECEPTACLE

DOOR 154L ◁ 1
FUEL CHECK PANEL

DOOR 47
LIFE HISTORY RECORDER

DOOR 15
LIQUID COOLANT SERVICING
ECS WATER SEPARATORS

DOOR 48L ◁ 2
FUEL CHECK PANEL

DOOR 79L
PC-1 RESERVOIR LEVEL INDICATOR

DOOR 39
(TOP SIDE)

LEFT MAIN WHEELWELL
PC-1 EXTERNAL CONNECTIONS
PC-1 RESERVOIR SERVICING

DOOR 45
AMMO LOADING

DOOR 40
(BOTTOM)
GUN SERVICE

DOOR 89L
JET FUEL STARTER
• HAND PUMP
• ACCUMULATOR PRESSURE GAGE
• ACCUMULATOR AIR CHARGE VALVE

DOOR 79R
PC-2 RESERVOIR LEVEL INDICATOR

DOOR 86L
AMAD OIL CHECK/SERVICING
IDG OIL CHECK/SERVICING
CGB OIL CHECK/SERVICING
MANUAL DECOUPLER HANDLE

RIGHT MAIN WHEELWELL
DEFUELING RECEPTACLE
PC-2 EXTERNAL CONNECTIONS
PC-2 RESERVOIR SERVICING

DOOR 89R
UTILITY EXTERNAL CONNECTIONS
UTILITY RESERVOIR SERVICING

DOOR 96L
EVENTS HISTORY RECORDER
(F100-PW-100)
ENGINE DIAGNOSTIC UNIT
(F100-PW-220)
• SIGHT GAGE
• SERVICING
  CONNECTIONS
• JOAP FITTING

DOOR 86R
AMAD OIL CHECK/SERVICING
IDG OIL CHECK

DOOR 96R
EVENTS HISTORY RECORDER
(F100-PW-100)
ENGINE DIAGNOSTIC UNIT
(F100-PW-220)
• SIGHT GAGE
• SERVICING
  CONNECTIONS
• JOAP FITTING

DOOR 111
FIRE EXTINGUISHER BOTTLE

DOOR 112
FIRE EXTINGUISHER PRESSURE GAGE
ARRESTING HOOK DAMPER PRESSURE GAGE

SPECIFICATIONS		USAF	NATO
FUEL	PRIMARY	MIL-T-5624, JP-4	. F-40
		MIL-T-83133, JP-8	F-34
	ALTERNATE	MIL-T-5624, JP-5	F-43 F-44
		JET A, JET A-1, JET B	F-35
EXTERNAL ELECTRICAL POWER		115±15 VAC, 400±30 Hz	A/M 32A-60A ONLY
HYDRAULIC FLUID		MIL-H-5606 MIL-H-83282	H-515 H-537
OXYGEN	LIQUID	MIL-O-27210	

SPECIFICATIONS		USAF	NATO
OIL	TURBINE ENGINE CENTRAL GEAR BOX INTEGRATED DRIVE GENERATOR AMAD	MIL-L-7808 (NO ALTERNATE)	O-148
NITROGEN	GASEOUS	BB-N-411 GRADE A, TYPE I OR II	
OIL	M61A1 GUN	MIL-L-46000	
EXTINGUISHING AGENT	FIRE EXTINGUISHER BOTTLE	HALON-1301	

1 ▷ F-15A/B AFTER TO 1F-15-1152 & ALL F-15C/D.
2 ▷ F-15A/B BEFORE TO 1F-15-1152.

15A-1-(22-1)9B-CATI

Figure 1-22. Servicing Diagram

Change 12
1-89/(1-90 blank)

Routine servicing is carried out in at least 24 different locations on the F-15. Notice the ammunition loading door (#45) in the bottom of the center fuselage. (U.S. Air Force)

On 1 May 1983, a simulated dogfight took place between two IDF/AF F-15Ds and four A-4N Skyhawks in the skies over the Negev. One of the F-15Ds (#957, nicknamed "Markia Shchakim," 4 kill marks) collided with one of the A-4s. The A-4 crashed, and the Eagle lost its right wing just outboard of the manufacturing joint where it attached to the fuselage. Although the F-15 initially entered a spin downward and to the right, the pilot quickly discovered that applying full afterburner provided sufficient thrust to keep the aircraft in the air and relatively stable. Touching down at 260 knots, the tail hook was used to snatch an arresting cable, slowing the F-15 to 100 knots. An emergency arresting net had been erected at the other end of the runway, but the pilot managed to brake the F-15 to a stop before impacting the net. McDonnell Douglas attributes the saving of this aircraft to the amount of lift generated by the engine intake/body and "... a hell of a good pilot." Two months later, the F-15 had been repaired and was returned to service, later scoring a fifth MiG kill. (Stefaan Vanhastel and Tsahi Ben-Ami Collections)

Mushayt, and No. 13 at King Abdul Aziz AFB at Dhahran.

On 5 June 1984 two Iranian F-4Es were shot down over the Persian Gulf by Saudi F-15s after receiving intercept instructions from an orbiting Boeing E-3A AWACS. This marked the first (and so far only known) encounter in which McDonnell-built aircraft fought each other.

US Congressional opposition to the delivery of further combat aircraft to Saudi Arabia and the Kingdom's desire to diversify its supply of military hardware led to a decision to order Panavia Tornados from Britain. However, in a move to ensure the continued availability of attrition aircraft, Saudi Arabia ordered 12 additional F-15C/Ds in early 1989. As with an Israeli order placed around the same time, these aircraft used the basic F-15E airframe since the original F-15C/D was no longer in production. The aircraft were to be stored in St. Louis, and dispatched to Saudi Arabia as needed to replace lost aircraft.

The Iraqi invasion of Kuwait on 2 August 1990 changed everything. The limit of only sixty F-15s in country at any one time was quickly dropped, and 20 additional F-15Cs (79-0015, 0017/0019, 0023/0024, 0028, 0031/0033, 0038/0039, 0043, 0045, 0051/0052, and 0055) and 4 F-15Ds (79-0004/0006 and 0010) were rushed to the RSAF from USAF stocks. These aircraft were "sanitized," and although they retain an ECM pod on top of the left vertical stabilizer, the ALQ-128 and ALQ-135 equipment itself was deleted. In

mid-1991, McDonnell began filling the 1989 order for nine additional F-15Cs (90-0263/0271) and three F-15Ds (90-0272/0274) that had been placed before the Gulf war began.

F-15S

In 1992, Saudi Arabia requested 24 additional F-15Fs, which were basically single-seat F-15Es without some of the more advanced avionics deemed too sensitive for export. The sale was rejected by the US Congress. Later in 1992, McDonnell Douglas proposed selling F-15H models, basically two-seat F-15Es lacking some of the more specialized capabilities, to Saudi Arabia. Again, the sale was rejected by Congress. Finally, on 10 May 1993, the RSAF was given permission to purchase 72 F-15XPs, slightly downgraded versions of the F-15E, currently known as the F-15S. The contract is estimated to be worth $9 billion, including equipment, maintenance, and support.

The F-15S is substantially similar to the F-15E, using F100-PW-229s, a slightly detuned APG-70 radar, and the F-15E "glass-cockpit." Forty-eight of the aircraft will be optimized for air-to-ground missions and will be equipped with LANTIRN pods, with the remainder being optimized for the air superiority role. The most readily apparent external difference is that the F-15S is painted a standard "Mod Eagle" scheme instead of the monotone gunship gray typical of the F-15E, and the lack of an ECM pod on top of the left vertical stabilizer.

Initially production was to be at a rate of two per month but budgetary pressures within the Kingdom have forced this to be halved to approximately one aircraft per month. The first F-15S made its initial flight on 19 June 1995, and was delivered to the RSAF in a ceremony at St. Louis on 12 September 1995. The remaining 71 aircraft are to be delivered by the end of 1999, along with conformal fuel tanks and LANTIRN systems for the 48 ground attack versions. The sale also includes 154 F100-PW-229 engines and various ground support equipment.

F-15U / F-15U(Plus)

This proposed version was designed to satisfy a requirement from the United Arab Emirates for 20-80 long-range interdiction aircraft. The F-15 was competing with the Lockheed Martin F-16, Dassault Rafale, Eurofighter 2000, and the Sukhoi Su-37MK. The original F-15U was basically an F-15E with systems tailored for the Emirates, including final assembly in the UAE. The F-15U(Plus) was a significantly upgraded aircraft, housing an additional 5,665 pounds of fuel in a thicker clipped-delta 50° leading-edge sweep wing, more weapon stations on the wings, and an internal LANTIRN installation. Typical ordnance loads included nine Mk 84 2,000-pound bombs, or seven laser-guided GBU-24s. The F-15 was eliminated in late-1996 when the UAE down-selected to the F-16 and Rafale. The UAE is expected to select a winner by the end of 1996, although the US Government has not yet reached a defense cooperation agreement with the Emirates, a fact that could ultimately restrict the sale of any US aircraft.

A version of the F-15U(Plus) has been proposed to South Korea, which is expected to place an order in 1999 for up to 120 new fighters. The "F-15K" (if the current designation strategy is maintained) would be co-produced in South Korea much like the F-16 (KFP-1). Again, the F-15 is in competition against the Su-37MK, but is the odds-on favorite at this early date.

This F-15A is not one of the four test aircraft that were transferred to the IDF/AF, evidenced by the large speedbrake and vertical tail pod configuration. It is unusual for the landing gear doors to be open except while the gear is cycling. (McDonnell Douglas)

ACRONYMS GALORE

Over the years, the F-15 has been modified literally hundreds of times. Some of these have been one-off test programs; other have been full-scale modification programs encompassing all USAF F-15s. As usual with government programs, most of these modifications have been known by arcane acronyms. There have also been various proposals for new versions of the F-15 to fill the reconnaissance and Wild Weasel roles, as well as versions for the US Navy, none of which were actually built.

F-15 MSIP

The Multi-Stage Improvement Program (MSIP) is a joint program carried out by McDonnell Douglas and the Air Force Warner Robins Logistics Center in Georgia. A MSIP-I for the F-15A/B was developed during 1982 in conjunction with the MSIP-II program for the F-15C/D, but MSIP-I was subsequently cancelled as uneconomical. Under the MSIP-II, upgrades were progressively incorporated onto the F-15C production line and then retrofitted to earlier production

F-15Cs. Although MSIP-I was cancelled, as of 1996 all F-15 versions (except the E) have gone through at least portions of MSIP, based on the condition of the airframe and other factors.

In February 1983 the Air Force awarded an $86.7 million contract to McDonnell Douglas for initial MSIP-II work, with a further $274.4 million released in December 1983. This covered the introduction of the Hughes APG-70 radar, upgrading the aircraft's central computer, replacing the cockpit armament panel with a single multi-purpose color display, new throttle grips and controls, a new video tape recorder split image control panel, and adding provisions for the Joint Tactical Information Distribution System.

Additionally, the capability to carry and launch the AIM-120A has been added. Other MSIP-II improvements include an enhanced electronic countermeasures suite consisting of an ALQ-135B internal countermeasures system, ALR-56C radar warning receiver, ALE-45 chaff/flare dispensers, and an enhanced ALQ-128 warning system. Another part of the MSIP was the Seek Talk program, which was designed to reduce the vulnerability of the UHF

An F-15C (86-0157) from Mountain Home's 390th FS shows the new shape of the ALQ-135B radome on the rear fuselage boom. Previously this radome was round, while on this aircraft (and several others) it has taken a more rectangular cross-section. There is nothing in the documentation that explains why the shape was changed, other than the obvious conclusion that the shape, and perhaps function, of the antenna inside has changed. This aircraft wears the so-called "Mod Eagle" paint scheme, which is generally similar to the original Compass Ghost scheme, but with more contrast between the two shades of gray. (Mick Roth)

radios to enemy jamming by introducing spread spectrum techniques and the use of a null steering antenna. The electronic systems resulted in a 25% improvement in reliability, with a corresponding increase in the readiness rate. Flight testing of the new systems began in December 1984, and the first F-15C (84-0001) to incorporate the changes was delivered on 20 June 1985.

F-15A/Bs that went through MSIP were not fitted with the APG-70 radar or conformal fuel tanks, but they are otherwise indistinguishable from MSIP-II F-15Cs. This includes the same late model main wheels that were one of the few distinguishing features of the later F-15s. The F-15A/Bs are now equipped with the same overload warning system as the F-15C/D which permits the pilot to maneuver safely to the 9g limit of the airframe at all design gross weights, eliminating the 7.33g restriction originally applied to the F-15A in certain flight

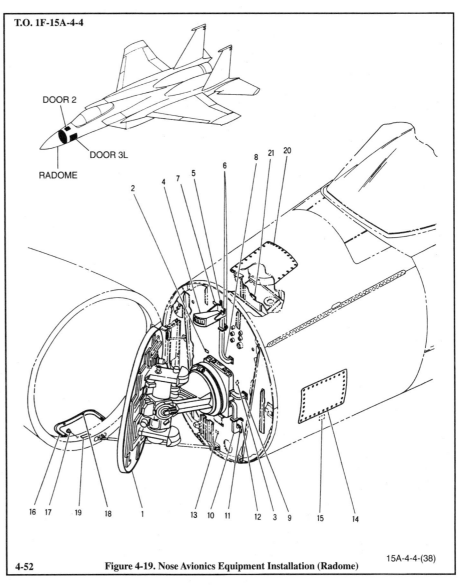

T.O. 1F-15A-4-4

DOOR 2
DOOR 3L
RADOME

4-52
Figure 4-19. Nose Avionics Equipment Installation (Radome)
15A-4-4-(38)

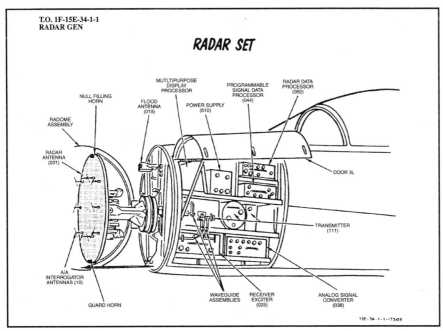

T.O. 1F-15E-34-1-1
RADAR GEN

RADAR SET

NULL FILLING HORN
RADOME ASSEMBLY
RADAR ANTENNA (031)
A/A INTERROGATOR ANTENNAS (10)
GUARD HORN
FLOOD ANTENNA (019)
MULTIPURPOSE DISPLAY PROCESSOR
POWER SUPPLY (610)
PROGRAMMABLE SIGNAL DATA PROCESSOR (044)
RADAR DATA PROCESSOR (082)
DOOR 3L
TRANSMITTER (111)
WAVEGUIDE ASSEMBLIES
RECEIVER EXCITER (025)
ANALOG SIGNAL CONVERTER (038)

15E-34-1-1-173(09)

The APG-63 and APG-70 radar sets use a 36-inch antenna in the extreme nose. This phased array antenna is capable of limited electronic steering, and is also fully articulated in both axes mechanically. A flood antenna (#4) is located on the aft bulkhead above the planer array. One of the ALQ-128 EWWS antennas (#14) is located on each side of the forward fuselage, with a third antenna on top of the left vertical stabilizer. Most of the electronic boxes for the radar system are located on either side of the fuselage directly behind the radome, and are accessible through large doors on each side. (U.S. Air Force)

Another Mountain Home F-15C (86-0158) shows the new forward fuselage ALQ-135B antennas. The speed brake is open to its full extension, and shows one of the major changes on the F-15 from the early test aircraft to operational units. Noteworthy is that the radome does not match the rest of the paint scheme, something that has become more prevalent in the mid-1990s. The radomes are replaced more frequently than the aircraft go through depot, so the paint on the radome is usually fresher. Interestingly, the rubberized portion at the tip is not painted, and they are all molded in either Compass Ghost or Gunship Gray and therefore none of them match the so-called "Mod Eagle" scheme. Recently, delamination of the composite radome, and even more so the speed brake, has become a problem. (Mick Roth)

NASA operates an F-15B (74-0141) as an Aerodynamic Flight Facility. The black Flight Test Facility (FTF-II) attached to the centerline station can accommodate a large variety of experiments. One of the first programs to use this aircraft was the X-33 reusable launch vehicle demonstrator, which tested thermal protection system concepts on the FTF-II. (Dennis R. Jenkins)

regimes. Instead of the APG-70, a new Hughes radar will be fitted to 350 earlier aircraft beginning in 1999, and will, in fact, replace some early versions of the APG-70.

Some of the very early F-15As (mainly from FY73-75) have not been upgraded under MSIP and will be retired and made available as gate guards or donated to museums. At least 20 of them reportedly will be given to Israel as payment for policy decisions made during the Gulf War, although since this has not accomplished by now tends to make it unlikely.

Although the scope of work defined by MSIP-II has been completed, various other modifications to the F-15 continue, and are generally considered an extension of MSIP. The most recent is a series of software updates, along with some minor hardware changes, under MSIP Suite 2M. These modifications include new software for the central computer, programmable armament control set, APG-63 radar, and JTIDS.

Although not technically part of MSIP, the Air Force is upgrading most F-15C/Ds to use the F100-PW-220E engine, which offers improved reliability and throttle

The Flight Test Facility on NASA's F-15B (74-0141). The pylon contains instrumentation, and provides a structure to hang experiments from. Otherwise, the F-15B is unmodified except for the removal of military subsystems and the addition of telemetry equipment. The main wheels are of the original F-15A/B design, and differ from the units currently fitted to most operational USAF aircraft. (Dennis R. Jenkins)

response. Originally the modification program was to upgrade approximately 250 engines per year and fit them into operational F-15s, but recent budget problems have reduced the rate to less than 55 engines per year.

F-15 ASAT

In 1979 a contract was issued to Vought for an anti-satellite (ASAT) vehicle to be launched from a modified F-15. The ASM-135A used a first stage derived from the AGM-69 SRAM-A and an Altair III second stage, was 17.81 feet long, and weighed approximately 2,700 pounds. A miniature kinetic kill vehicle used an infrared seeker to home in on the target satellite,

The 412th Test Wing operates several F-15s for continued operational test and evaluation. This F-15A (74-0116) was shown with a full complement of AIM-120 AMRAAM missiles at the Edwards airshow in 1996. Unusually, it carries no ALQ-135 antennas on the forward fuselage or tail booms. The paint scheme is typical of the "Mod Eagle," which is officially referred to as the "High and Low Reflectance Gray" scheme. (Dennis R. Jenkins)

The F-15S/MTD (71-0290) shows off its unusual two-dimensional exhaust nozzles. These nozzles could deflect thrust upwards or downwards as much as 20 degrees. The louvers ahead of the nozzles allowed thrust reversing, a technique that proved useful in reducing the F-15's landing distance to as little as 1,366 feet. These nozzles pioneered much of the technology being used by the F-22's nozzles, although the F-15 ACTIVE's nozzles probably represent a better thrust-vectoring system. (AFFTC History Office)

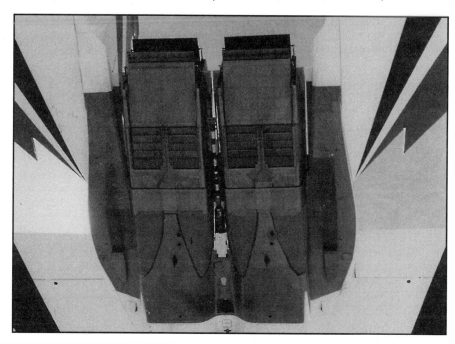

Many of the modifications made to 71-0290 to convert it into the F-15S/MTD were essentially the same as the proposed modifications for the F-15E (which had not yet entered production). Beefier landing gear, a glass-cockpit, and an APG-70 radar were added. The aircraft, however, still used the original small speed brake typical of the first 20 aircraft. The canards are modified F/A-18 stabilators. (AFFTC History Office)

destroying it completely by impact, and no explosive warhead was fitted.

An F-15A (76-0086) was modified for trials with the ASM-135A which was intended to be launched against an orbiting satellite after a zoom climb to 80,000 feet. The ASM-135A was carried on the centerline station of the F-15 which was specially wired and provided with a backup battery, microprocessor, and datalink for mid-course guidance housed within a special centerline pylon. Beginning in the early 1980s, captive flights were made with the missile in place, and the first launch took place in January 1984, the missile being aimed at a predetermined point in space. Subsequently, three launches of the ASM-135A were made against celestial infrared sources.

The first and only ASM-135A launch against an actual satellite target took place on 13 September 1985, when an F-15A (77-0084) of the 6512th Test Squadron took off from Vandenberg AFB, zoom-climbed to 80,000 feet, then launched the ASAT against the Solwind P78-1, a gamma ray spectroscopy satellite that had been launched in February 1979. Both the first and second stages fired successfully, and the miniature kinetic kill vehicle separated and homed in on the satellite, destroying it upon impact. This test enraged arms control advocates, who saw the test as a violation of a joint US/Soviet treaty forbidding the development and testing of anti-satellite weapons. Solar scientists were not happy about the test either, since although the Solwind P78-1 had officially completed its mission, it was still sending back useful data.

Initial plans were to modify twenty F-15As for the anti-satellite mission and to assign them to the 48th FIS at Langley AFB and the 318th FIS at McChord AFB. These squadrons had each received three or four of the modified F-15As before Congress became unwilling to permit any further testing of the system, and the ASAT program was officially terminated in 1988. The modifications did not affect the operational usage of the F-15s *(text continued on page 69)*

The NF-15B ACTIVE research aircraft (71-0290). This is the second configuration for the thrust-vectoring F-15, having originally carried two-dimensional rectangular nozzles. The ACTIVE successfully performed the fastest known thrust-vectoring at Mach 2.0 on 31 October 1996. (NASA / Dryden)

THE EAGLE'S PLUMAGE

NOT TOTALLY GRAY

For as superior a fighter as the F-15 is, it has to rank as one of the world's most boring aircraft to look at as far as paint schemes go. The first 42 F-15s were painted in "air-superiority" blue, with the exception of 71-0287 which was finished in gloss white for its role as the spin-test aircraft, and 72-0119 (Streak Eagle) which was not painted. Air Superiority Blue (officially, simply "Superiority Blue") consisted of the upper surfaces being painted in a gloss AS Blue (FS35450) and the lower surfaces getting flat AS Blue (FS15450). This paint scheme was considered effective in the clear blue skies over Edwards and Luke, but it was not so effective in cloudy skies, such as those expected to be encountered over Europe.

Early production aircraft after 73-0100 (74-0137 for two-seaters), including foreign deliveries, have been painted in "Compass Ghost." Project Compass Ghost has been a continuing effort by the military to find the most effective camouflage scheme possible. The standard F-15

For four days in April 1976, the second TF-15A (71-0291) was painted in French air force markings for demonstration flights. Unfortunately, the French decided against purchasing the Eagle, leaving this as the only "French" F-15. The flags under the cockpit represent various countries that the F-15 had been demonstrated to in an attempt to secure purchases. The early test aircraft usually had black tips on their radomes, a left-over from initial plans to paint the radomes black like the F-4 and other earlier fighters. The tips are molded in their color, and were too far into production to change when the decision to paint the radomes was made. (Dennis R. Jenkins)

The fourth test F-15A (71-0283) displays its brand new day-glo orange markings at the NASA/Dryden open house in May 1973. The orange generally faded in the intense desert sun, and seldom did the early aircraft look this good. The horizontal black stripes on the vertical stabilizers were unique to this aircraft. The large cylinder on the nose boom protects the instru- mentation from the general public (and vice versa). The national insignia on the forward fuselage is unusual since it has a dark outline: most test aircraft and early operational aircraft omitted the outline. (Dennis R. Jenkins)

scheme prior to 1990 consisted of two shades of gray, called Light Ghost Gray (FS36320) and Dark Ghost Gray (FS36375), applied in a pattern designed to minimize the visual reflectance of various contours of the aircraft. The exception to this is the F-15E, all of which have been painted a monotone, very dark Gunship Gray (FS36114). The four short-lived ADTAC fighter interceptor squadrons were the only units that consistently applied colorful unit markings.

Despite all the modifications that 71-0290 has been through, it still retains the original small speed brake typical of the early test aircraft. The bulges that house the actuators for the forward canards are clearly visible above the intakes. The canards did not affect the refueling receptacle in the left wing root, but prohibit carrying the M61 cannon in the right wing root. (NASA / Dryden)

It is somewhat unusual to see F-15Es with AIM-7s on the conformal fuel tanks, although it is entirely possible to carry four of them. Here 88-1691 is shown with an AIM-7 on each aft CFT station, and two Sidewinders under each wing. The mismatch on the radome color is very noticeable, as are the plethora of "remove before flight" tags hanging from the aircraft. (Jerry Langston via the Mick Roth Collection)

An excellent portrait of a current 1st FW F-15C (83-0033). The "Mod Eagle" paint scheme is typical of mid-1990s practice, although the tail codes are unusually bright (and slightly crooked) to highlight that this is a commander's aircraft. A full complement of air-to-air missiles are loaded, with an AIM-7 on the forward air intake position, and AIM-120s on the aft fuselage and also on the outboard wing rail, and, mostly hidden, an AIM-9 on the inboard wing rail. The standard 610-gallon fuel tank is hung on the centerline. Red plastic protective covers have been installed over all the grilles pitot/alpha sensors. (Don Logan)

WARBIRDTECH
SERIES

Beginning in the late 1980s, Compass Ghost was replaced by the "High and Low Reflectance Gray" scheme that uses two new shades of gray (FS36251 and FS 36176). This so-called "Mod Eagle" scheme has been applied to almost all air superiority F-15s as they progress through depot-level maintenance or the MSIP program, and is also standard on the F-15S aircraft destined for Saudi Arabia, and F-15Is for Israel.

This F-15A (73-0103) at Luke was painted in high-visibility red and white "invasion stripes" as a test during early 1976 to find a more visible paint scheme for the Eagle during transition training at Luke. Note that the fuselage stripes sweep back, unlike the black and white scheme where the stripes were vertical. This scheme, like the others tested, was not adopted for use. (Mick Roth)

In mid-1976, four F-15s (including 74-0139) were painted in attitude deceptive paint schemes developed by noted aviation artist Keith Ferris. Each aircraft was slightly different, using various shades of gray and different geometric patterns. Although the scheme proved fairly successful in initially confusing the opposing pilots, it also allowed the aircraft to be spotted at longer ranges. Similar schemes were tested on F-14 and T-38 aircraft, but none were adopted for operational use. (Jim Rotramel)

The No. 204 Squadron (7th Air Wing) celebrated the squadron's 30th anniversary, along with the 10th anniversary (1991) of the F-15's introduction into JASDF service with this specially painted F-15J (32-8826). This aircraft shows two unique modifications made to JASDF F-15s. The first is the Japanese J/ALQ-8 antennas under the nose, between the two UHF blade antennas that are covered by "remove before flight" tags. This system is roughly equivalent to the ALQ-135 system carried on American F-15s. The second are two small air probes or cooling scoops that show up immediately below the air intakes. The purpose of these is unknown, but they only appear on aircraft that have the ALQ-8 antennas, so it is believed they are related to that system. (Dennis R. Jenkins Collection)

The 350th F-15C (85-0125) on the assembly line in St. Louis. The different colors of the various alloys used in making the skin panels is noteworthy. At this stage, the wings are being attached to the center fuselage, which in turn is attached to the aft and forward fuselage sections. The horizontal stabilizers are attached at the next assembly line station. (McDonnell Douglas)

Among the exceptions to "boring" F-15 paint schemes are the six F-15DJs assigned to the Japanese aggressor squadron (Hiko Kyodotai) based at Nyutabaru. Each of these Eagles has a unique camouflage scheme, such as 02-8072 seen here. (Masahiro Koizumi)

The third high-visibility test aircraft from Luke in April 1976 used yellow bands on the tails and wings. This F-15A (73-0100) was the first aircraft delivered in Compass Ghost instead of air-superiority blue. Overall the visual effect of the yellow bands was very pleasing, and it is unfortunate that the scheme was not adapted for operational use. All early Luke aircraft used white tail codes, except 73-0109, which used black tail codes for several months prior to switching to white. Most later F-15 squadrons used black tail codes from the beginning. Note the early pod configuration on the top of the vertical stabilizers. (Dave Begy)

(text continued from page 64)
although the wiring and other changes were removed as the aircraft went through the MSIP program.

IFFC/Firefly III F-15

In February 1982 McDonnell Douglas was awarded a 15 month contract by the Air Force Flight Dynamics Laboratory (FDL) to demonstrate an advanced integrated flight control/fire control system under the Integrated Flight-Fire Control (IFFC) program. An F-15B's (77-0166) fire control and flight control systems were modified to accept control inputs from both the pilot and the IFFC computer and to tailor flight control response to the various weapons delivery modes. The IFFC allowed a sensor locked on a target to effectively fly the aircraft to weapons release or gun firing posi-

ACTIVE's new thrust-vectoring nozzles do not look particularly different than the normal F100 nozzles. However, they provide the ability to vector thrust up to 20 degrees in any direction, and have successfully demonstrated this capability throughout the F-15's flight envelope. Unlike the original two-dimensional nozzles used on the F-15S/MTD, it would be possible to retrofit the new nozzles to either the F-15 or F-16 with relatively minor modifications. (NASA / Dryden)

tion. During test flights, air-to-air weapons were fired at simulated targets while the F-15 was maneuvered at high offset angles, demonstrating its ability to employ weapons accurately while in three-dimensional flight. A parallel Firefly III program was conducted by General Electric for further development of the fire control system.

The coupling of IFFC with Firefly III allowed automatic positioning of the aircraft in order to attack targets that are detected by an electro-optical target designation pod. As part of the program, the F-15B carried a Martin Marietta Automatic Tracking Laser Illumination System (ALTIS II) pod on the forward port-side AIM-7 station, linked to the aircraft's fly-by-wire system. The designation pod enabled the aircraft to release air-to-ground weapons while maneuvering along a three-dimensional flight path, avoiding having to fly directly over the target and thus exposing itself to enemy ground fire.

The F-15 was the first major USAF fighter to have a wraparound windscreen (no center supports), although some smaller aircraft such as the F-5 had already pioneered the concept. One of the changes made during the F-15's production run was the introduction of a slightly different windscreen on the F-15E. The original windscreen did not have the small filet in the bottom corner, and had exposed screws around the entire base. It suffered from cracking due to thermal cycles where the stretched acrylic met the fiberglass frame. Interestingly, the F-15's maximum speed is not determined by the amount of thrust or aerodynamic drag, but by the speed at which the windscreen begins to become soft (melt). This translates to somewhere around Mach 2.3, depending upon conditions. (Todd Enlund)

The trust-vectoring capabilities of ACTIVE's engines are shown here. The left engine is deflected downward, while the right engine is in a neutral position. The small speed brake is again evident, shown here in its fully extended position. (NASA / Dryden)

Although the IFFC/Firefly III system was never adopted for production F-15s, the work accomplished on the system was helpful during integration of LANTIRN into the F-15E Strike Eagle.

F-15 S/MTD

On 3 October 1984, the FDL awarded a $117.8 million cost-sharing contract to McDonnell Douglas for the development of an advanced Short Take-Off and Landing/Maneuvering Technology Demonstrator (S/MTD) experimental aircraft. The basic idea was to develop an aircraft that could land and take off from sections of wet, bomb-damaged runway under bad-weather conditions and severe crosswinds, and without active ground-based navigational assistance. The first two-seat F-15B (71-0290) was selected for modification as the S/MTD demonstrator under project Agile Eagle.

Changes included controllable canards, modified from F/A-18A stabilators, mounted on the engine inlet trunks forward of the wings. The foreplanes were mounted at a dihedral angle of 20˚, and could operate symmetrically or asymmetrically to provide pitch and roll moments. They were used as stability maintaining surfaces instead of for primary flight control and, in theory, permitted the F-15B's maximum allowable load factor to be increased above 9g without additional structural reinforcement. The aircraft was also fitted with F-15E landing gear and glass cockpit.

The Integrated Flight/Propulsion Control (IFPC) system was developed by McDonnell Douglas and produced by General Electric. The IFPC managed all control parameters and was intended to relieve the pilot of some of the more routine tasks of handling the aircraft. There were five modes of operation: conventional, short take-off/approach, short landing, cruise, and combat. The modified aircraft flew for the first time on 7 September 1988 with McDonnell Douglas test pilot Larry Walker at the controls, and a total of 43 test flights were carried out in this configuration.

The spin-test aircraft (71-0287) was turned over to NASA and assigned the tail number 835. This aircraft had always been painted white, so little was needed to make it look like a NASA aircraft. It was used for a variety of engine and control systems tests, and is currently used as a source of spare parts to keep other NASA F-15s flying. (NASA / Dryden)

WARBIRD**TECH**
SERIES

One of two F-15As (76-0086) modified to launch the Vought ASM-135A anti-satellite missile (ASAT). The original plan was to equip two of the fighter interceptor squadrons with the capability to carry and launch the missile to provide a limited anti-satellite capability against Soviet low-earth orbit reconnaissance satellites. The missile was carried on the centerline station, and was launched against a real satellite only once before Congress halted development.
(Dennis R. Jenkins)

In the second phase of the program, the standard convergent-divergent engine nozzles were replaced with rectangular two-dimensional thrust-vectoring nozzles. These nozzles were built by Pratt & Whitney out of chemically-milled and welded titanium honeycomb. They had flat upper and lower flaps that were independently driven and capable of adjusting the exhaust upwards or downwards as much as 20°. There were a set of vanes above and below the nozzle that made it possible for the thrust to be reversed.

The first flight with the thrust-vectoring nozzles took place on 16 May 1989 in St. Louis, and the aircraft was subsequently flown to Edwards. The first in-flight vectoring occurred on 23 March 1990. Test flights demonstrated that the thrust-vectoring features of the new nozzles worked as anticipated and resulted in a 25 percent reduction in takeoff roll, and the thrust-reversing feature made it possible for the F-15 to land in 1,650 feet, and also allowed rapid deceleration during flight, a useful feature during close-in air-to-air combat. During the test program, the F-15 S/MTD made numerous vectored takeoffs with rotation demonstrated at speeds as low as 42 mph. The shortest landing took only 1,366 feet, compared to a basic F-15's 7,500 feet.

The program ended on 15 August 1991 after accomplishing all of its flight objectives. The vectored thrust nozzles were returned to Pratt & Whitney, although the aircraft itself would be called upon for further flight tests of yet another vectored thrust system as the F-15 ACTIVE.

NF-15B ACTIVE

The NF-15B ACTIVE (Advanced Control Technology for Integrated Vehicles) project uses the same F-15B (71-0290) previously modified by the S/MTD program. ACTIVE is intended to develop and demonstrate flight control technologies that will significantly enhance the

The eighth test aircraft (71-0287) was assigned to the Digital Electronic Engine Control program in an attempt to cure the persistent stall/stagnation problem the F-15 was experiencing. The results of these tests were used to finalize the electronic engine controls introduced on the F100-PW-220 engine. The small speed brake is at approximately 40% of its maximum extension. This aircraft was later bailed to NASA for various tests.
(Dennis R. Jenkins)

operational characteristics for the next generation of high performance aircraft. ACTIVE is a joint NASA, Air Force, McDonnell Douglas Aerospace, and P&W program. The flight test program will encompass approximately 60 flights totaling 100 hours.

Externally, the aircraft is configured much like the S/MTD demonstrator, except that the two-dimensional thrust-vectoring nozzles have been replaced by two F100-PW-229s with multi-directional thrust-vectoring nozzles. The engines have modified fan duct cases to provide the additional strength required to withstand the vectoring forces. Installation of the nozzles also required modifications to the aircraft's rear fuselage and main engine mounts.

The Vought ASM-135A anti-satellite weapon was a large missile based on a SRAM rocket motor. A modified centerline pylon still allowed sufficient ground clearance during ground operations. The weapon was only fired against an actual satellite once, and it scored a direct hit. Plans involved equipping two fighter interceptor squadrons with modified F-15As, but Congress cancelled the program after only a handful of aircraft had been delivered. (Dennis R. Jenkins)

The new nozzles are officially known as pitch-yaw balance beam nozzles, and can be vectored up to ±20° in any direction. The nozzle features a fail-safe dual redundant actuation system, making it compatible with single-engine, as well as twin-engine, applications. Unlike the two-dimensional nozzles used on the S/MTD, these nozzles are not equipped with thrust reversers. A similar pitch-yaw vectoring nozzle

Almost all F-15s have had the original rear fuselage fairing removed, leaving the tail hook exposed. All F-15Es were initially delivered in this configuration. The F-15E does not have the door covering the tail hook, but most earlier models retained the door, even after the deletion of the fairing. Like most Air Force aircraft, this tail hook is meant for contingency landings only, and is not as robust as the arresting hooks found on Navy aircraft intended for carrier landings. (Todd Enlund)

WARBIRD**TECH**
S E R I E S

has been selected for integration into a modified F-16D in the Air Force's Variable-stability In-flight Simulator Test Aircraft (VISTA).

Initial test flights centered on defining normal aircraft operations with the new nozzles and flight software. Slow-speed thrust vectoring tests were then accomplished, and on 24 April 1996 the F-15 ACTIVE achieved its first supersonic yaw vectoring flight at Dryden. The first vectoring at Mach 2 occurred on 31 October 1996, and was accomplished by NASA test pilot Jim Smolka at 45,000 feet. This was the first known Mach 2 trust vectoring by any aircraft, and effectively completed opening the flight envelope for ACTIVE. Testing is scheduled to continue into 1997, including additional supersonic vectoring demonstrations.

F-15s WITH NASA

The second F-15A (71-0281) was acquired by the NASA Dryden Flight Research Center on 17 December 1975, and was used for the aerodynamic testing of the space shuttle's thermal protection tiles. The tiles attached to the starboard wing simulated those on the leading edge of the orbiter's wing, whereas those on the port wing simulated those on the junction of the orbiter's wing and fuselage. The tiles attached to the F-15A's wing were ultimately subjected to almost 1.5 times the dynamic pressure which the Shuttle experiences during launch. Various other minor test programs were carried out using 71-0281. The aircraft was returned to the USAF on 28 October 1983 without being assigned a NASA number, and is now on display at Langley AFB.

An ALQ-128 antenna is on top of the left vertical stabilizer, while a mass balancer is located on the right tail. These pods have changed several times over the production run of the Eagle. Early test aircraft had pods similar to the ALQ-128 pod located on both tails, although there was not a rounded radome on the rear of the pod. Early operational aircraft had a similar configuration. All foreign aircraft only have mass balancers on each tail, except for the USAF F-15C/Ds that were hurriedly transferred to Saudi Arabia during the Gulf war. (Dennis R. Jenkins)

The raised white letters are optional, and usually only done for air shows. The main landing gear wheels have been changed several times during the F-15's lifetime. This is the latest wheel, and features eight holes. Earlier wheels had either 12 holes, or a series of triangular openings. The wheels were painted black for most of the Eagle's career, but by the mid-1990s they began to be painted white to make inspecting them for cracks easier. (Dennis R. Jenkins)

The nose landing gear is fairly simple in construction, and contains landing lights mounted on the forward strut, and one (of two) landing gear doors attached to the back of the strut. The larger of the two doors is hinged on the fuselage, and is normally closed except while the landing gear is in motion. (Dennis R. Jenkins)

The eighth F-15A (71-0287) was acquired by DFRC on 5 January 1976 and received NASA number 835. This highly-instrumented one-of-a-kind aircraft, known as the F-15 Flight Research Facility, was equipped with an integrated digital propulsion-flight control system. Flight research carried out by NASA with this F-15 evaluated advanced integrated flight and propulsion control system technologies during more than 25 advanced research projects involving aerodynamics, performance, propulsion control, control integration, instrumentation development, human factors, and flight test techniques.

During 1982 and early-1983, NASA tested a digital electronic engine control (DEEC) advanced fuel management system in support of the F100-PW-220 development aboard 71-0287. The system was based on microprocessor control of the gas generator and afterburner control units in an attempt to finally cure the F100's tendency to stagnate or stall at certain throttle settings in particular flight regimes. During the summer of 1983, 71-0287 was used in a further series of demonstrations for the Engine Model Derivative (EMD, later called the Improved Performance Engine—IPE). These tests demonstrated that relatively modest engine improvements could drastically improve performance: acceleration from Mach 0.8 to Mach 2.0 was improved 41 percent at 35,000 feet, as well as improved airstart capabilities and better specific fuel consumption figures.

NASA 835 was later used in the development the Highly Integrated Electronic Control (HIDEC) system; Advanced Digital Engine Control System (ADECS); Self-Repairing

The second F-15A (71-0281) was used by NASA for various research programs, including evaluating Space Shuttle thermal protection system tiles. Tiles were mounted on the starboard wing and the port wing extension, with a smooth surface being achieved with the liberal use of body putty. Surprisingly, this aircraft's wingtip had not been modified to the raked configuration prior to it being bailed to NASA. (NASA/Dryden)

Flight Control System (SRFCS); Performance Seeking Control (PSC); and Propulsion Controlled Aircraft (PCA) system. The NASA F-15 was the first aircraft to demonstrate a fully integrated inlet-engine-flight control system, a self-repairing flight control system, and a propulsion-only flight control system. It was also used as a testbed to evaluate aerodynamic pressures on Space Shuttle thermal protection tiles at specific altitudes and speeds. NASA 835, in a beautiful white and blue paint scheme, is currently (1997) being used for spare parts to keep NASA 836 and the F-15/ACTIVE flying.

Beginning in 1994, NASA started flying an F-15B (74-0141) as the Aerodynamic Flight Facility designated NASA 836. The Flight Test Fixture-II (FTF-II) is installed on the centerline pylon in a manner similar to the normal centerline tank. The FTF-II is a low-aspect-ratio structure that is 107 inches long, 32 inches high, and 8 inches wide with a 12° elliptical nose section and blunt trailing edge. Built primarily of carbon-epoxy materials, the fixture consists of a pylon with replaceable side panels, nose section, and vertical test article. The modular configuration allows the FTF-II to be modified to satisfy a variety of flight test requirements. The upper 19 inches of the FTF-II is the permanent pylon that houses avionics, research instrumentation systems, and other support equipment common to most flight experiments. The lower 13 inches of the FTF-II is the vertical test article that, in the current configuration, matches the contour of the upper avionics pylon. The vertical test article is removable and may be replaced by other aerodynamic shapes.

In 1996 DFRC completed flight testing of the X-33 thermal protection system using the F-15B/FTF-II. These tests provided information on the material's durability at flight velocities through adverse weather, much like the tests conducted with the Space Shuttle tiles 11 years earlier.

TESTBEDS AND OTHER IDEAS

In May 1971 McDonnell Douglas received a contract to develop a composite wing for the F-15 consisting of boron and graphite filaments embedded in epoxy resin. The wing was 500 pounds lighter and had a longer fatigue life than the metal wing used in production

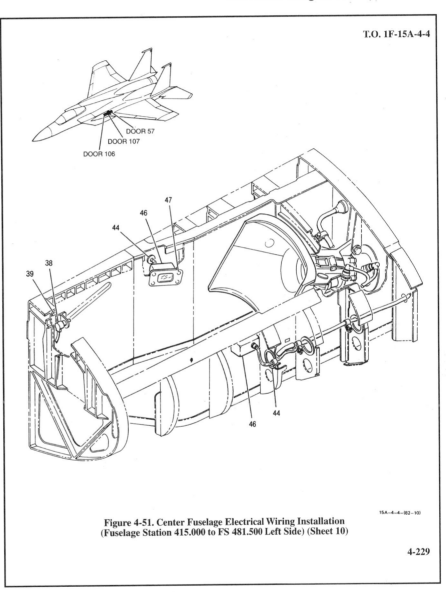

T.O. 1F-15A-4-4

DOOR 57
DOOR 107
DOOR 106

47
46
44
38
39

44
46

15A-4-4-(82-10)

Figure 4-51. Center Fuselage Electrical Wiring Installation (Fuselage Station 415.000 to FS 481.500 Left Side) (Sheet 10)

4-229

The F-15's refueling receptacle is located in the left wing root. Two lights illuminate the receptacle for the boom operator on the tanker. All F-15s, including foreign sales, have included the receptacle, and no provisions exist for fitting a probe-and-drogue system to the fighter. Like most USAF aircraft, an emergency system is provided that enables the pilot to explosively open the refueling door in the event the mechanical systems fail. (U.S. Air Force)

aircraft. Structural test articles were completed and flight tests were scheduled for late-1975. Unfortunately the project was cancelled in February 1975, but the technology found uses in the F/A-18A and AV-8B. A subsequent project did result in the first F-15B (71-0290) flying with aluminum-lithium (Al-Li) wing panels which are five percent stronger and nine percent lighter then the conventional aluminum panels they replace. Flight tests started in the summer of 1986, and are continuing aboard 71-0290 in its role as the F-15/ACTIVE demonstrator. Although never adopted for production on the F-15, these tests did prove the worth of this new lightweight metal for use on high performance aircraft.

In 1974 McDonnell Douglas received a $6 million contract from the Flight Dynamics Laboratory to design and build an advanced environmental control system for use in the F-15. The Air Force had evaluated aircraft electronic system failures and found that 52 percent of them were directly related to temperature, humidity, or dust. McDonnell Douglas developed a high-capacity cooling system, complete with dust separators and a dehumidifier, which in addition to maintaining lower temperatures in the electronics, also reduced windscreen fog, and provided a more comfortable cockpit. The system was flight tested aboard an F-15A (71-0282) during 1978, and some aspects of the system were incorporated into the F-15C/D.

Another attempt at decreasing the structural weight of the aircraft was made on 11 October 1985 when McDonnell Douglas received a contract from ASD for the construction of two composite horizontal stabilizers, one for static tests and the other for ground vibration tests after a limited flight test series on the first F-15B (71-0290). The program started in February 1986 and was completed in September 1986. Each torque box consisted of a substructure made of superplastically-formed and diffusion bonded titanium with the skins consisting of boron fiber composite coated with boron carbide. The leading and trailing edges were made of superplastically-formed aluminum to avoid corrosion. The project demonstrated a 50 percent cost

The McDonnell Douglas demonstrator (71-0291) was used to demonstrate advanced reconnaissance concepts during 1987. Although not shown here, the aircraft was usually fitted with a semi-conformal reconnaissance pod under the centerline, and proved it could be a very capable, if overly expensive, replacement for the RF-4C. Unfortunately, it was not procured, and 71-0291 went on to become the Strike Eagle demonstrator. Barely visible here is a placard on the wing root extension that identifies it as being constructed of aluminum-lithium alloy, one of several areas of the F-15 that were tested with the advanced lightweight alloy. (Daniel Soulaine via the Mick Roth Collection)

WARBIRDTECH
SERIES

Several F-15s are maintained at Edwards AFB by the 412th Test Wing for continued testing, and also for use as chase aircraft. A couple, such as this F-15B (75-0134), have been painted in gloss white with high-visibility orange trim on the vertical stabilizers and wings. Although the normal pod is on top of the left fin, the actual ALQ-128 radome is missing from the aft end of it. In fact, all ECM antennas are missing from this aircraft. (Craig Kaston via the Mick Roth Collection)

reduction over the current machined titanium substructure, and also yielded a 17 percent weight reduction. Many of the techniques learned were subsequently applied to the F-15E program.

F-15N

McDonnell Douglas defined several naval variants of the F-15 from 1970 to 1974 and an unofficial (and perhaps, unwelcome) title of "Seagle" was applied by various organizations involved. The first presentation to the Navy occurred in July 1971. McDonnell Douglas's position was that due to its excellent thrust-to-weight ratio and good visibility, the F-15 could be adapted for carrier operations. The only modifications required to enable it to operate off of CVA-19 class carriers were: strengthened landing gear; an extendible front landing gear strut to produce the proper angle of attack upon catapult launch; instal-

lation of a nose-tow catapult system; folding wings; and a beefed-up arresting hook and associated structure. Both the nose and main landing gear wells would have to be enlarged to accommodate the increased stroke of the new gear. These modifications would have added approximately 2,300 pounds to the basic F-15A.

The Navy was not overly impressed with this proposal, so McDonnell Douglas presented two more extensively modified models (199A-11A and 199A-12). Model 199A-12 featured a bridle catapult attachment, while 199A-11A had a nose-tow catapult attachment, but otherwise they were identical. The design also featured a dual nose wheel, increased fuselage structural strength, a Navy-type refueling probe, and most important, an improved high-lift system. The high-lift system was composed of full-span leading edge flaps, BLC trailing edge flaps, and a slotted

aileron, all of which contributed 632 pounds to the projected 3,055 pound increase (to 42,824 pounds) over the F-15A.

The F-15N then became the subject of Navy Fighter Study Group III which disregarded the McDonnell Douglas data, enlarged the nose to carry the AWG-9 radar, and added Phoenix missiles resulting in an aircraft that weighed 10,000 pounds more than the basic F-15A. This weight increase, along with the associated drag, greatly decreased the performance of the F-15, negating any advantage it had over the F-14A. There was also considerable concern over the 12° angle-of-attack used by the F-15 (compared to 10.2° for the F-14A) during approaches, and the relatively narrow-track of the Eagle's landing gear.

McDonnell Douglas and Hughes countered the study group's criticisms with a further modified ver-

Looking in the air intake towards the engine. The area deep inside the intake is painted white to eliminate a "black hole" phenomenon that makes the aircraft easier to see from head-on. It also makes it easier for ground crews to identify FOD (foreign object debris/damage) that might have accidentally gotten into the intake. (Todd Enlund)

sion (199A-19B) known as F-15(N-PHX), which added a rudimentary AIM-54 Phoenix missile capability. The aircraft could carry up to eight AIM-54s: one on each fuselage AIM-7 station, one on each inboard wing pylon, and two (in tandem) on a special centerline pylon. The high-lift devices were changed to include full-span Krueger leading edge flaps, BLC trailing edge flaps, and single-slotted ailerons. Take-off weight was up to 46,009 pounds, and approach speed was estimated at 136 knots.

On 30 March 1973, the Senate Armed Services Committee's ad hoc Tactical Air Power subcommittee started new discussions on the possibilities of modifying the F-15 for the Navy mission. At this point the F-14 program was having difficulties, and the subcommittee wanted to look at possible alterna-

tives, namely lower-cost (stripped) F-14Ts, F-15Ns, and improved F-4s. These discussions, along with some other considerations, led to the forming of Navy Fighter Study Group IV, out of which the aircraft ultimately known as F/A-18A was born. No Navy F-15 variant was ever produced.

F-15XX

In September 1985, the USAF issued an RFP for an Advanced Tactical Fighter (ATF) that would be capable of supersonic cruise with a range greater than that of the F-15. It was to take maximum advantage of stealth technology consistent with its primary performance goals. McDonnell Douglas teamed with Northrop in building two YF-23 prototypes but on 23 April 1991, the Secretary of the Air Force announced that the competing

Lockheed/Boeing YF-22 had been selected as the winner. Current plans are for the F-15 to be gradually replaced in service by the F-22A, but given the budgetary constraints and progress of the F-22 FSD program, this will not begin to happen until 2005 at the earliest.

After the F-22 announcement, McDonnell Douglas submitted an unsolicited proposal to the Air Force Systems Command for a stripped down F-15 known as the F-15XX. It was considered as a possible low-cost alternative to the ATF, which has a current price tag of almost $100 million per aircraft. However, the Air Force did not want to appear to waiver on its support of F-22, and no work was ever authorized on the F-15XX proposal.

RF-15 / F-15(R)

Very early in the F-15 program, McDonnell Douglas proposed a reconnaissance variant. There were several variations to this theme including one with a special nose with camera ports, similar in concept to that employed on the RF-4B/C. This version also employed a TV camera, multi-spectral scanner, and side-looking radar in a modified lower fuselage. The Air Force did not have the funds to pursue the idea.

As a private venture McDonnell Douglas developed a conformal reconnaissance pod designed to be carried instead of the centerline stores station of two-seat F-15s under the internal F-15(R) "Peep Eagle" program. The pod was flight tested in the summer of 1987 aboard the second F-15B (71-0291). The Reconnaissance Technology Demonstrator pod could carry a full range of camera and imaging

equipment and was capable of transmitting imagery data to ground stations directly. A lack of funds precluded any further work on this project.

On 19 April 1995 an F-15D first flew carrying a Loral-Fairchild ATARS sensor pod on the centerline pylon. Only two flights were made with this configuration, but sufficient data was gathered to prove the concept. However, based largely on cost, the F-16 is more likely to be chosen for the reconnaissance mission.

F-15G WILD WEASEL

McDonnell Douglas has periodically proposed a version of the two-seat F-15 as the heir-apparent to the F-4G Advanced Wild Weasel defense suppression aircraft. The McDonnell Douglas demonstrator F-15B (71-0291) was flight tested with an aerodynamic pod under its nose, vaguely reminiscent of the F-4G chin pod, that was intended to hold the APR-38 Wild Weasel system. While generally endorsed by the USAF, the expense of the aircraft make its adoption for this role seem unlikely. Nevertheless, in May 1986, McDonnell Douglas received a $500,000 ten-month study contract for continued development under the "Wild Weasel VII" nomenclature, although no production contract was forthcoming.

In 1994, the USAF awarded yet another contract ($21 million in FY94, $37.4 million in FY95) to McDonnell Douglas to explore the feasibility of adapting the F-15C to the Suppression of Enemy Air Defenses (SEAD) role, replacing the F-4G. As part of the program, it was proposed to modify F-15Cs to fire the AGM-88 HARM anti-radiation missile with additional avionics for the SEAD role provided in distinctive "cheek" fairings. However, based mainly on its lower cost, specially modified F-16Cs were chosen as the SEAD platform, and the F-15 Wild Weasel never made it past a paper study. The Air Force continues to be interested in the concept however, and it could make a return at a later date if the F-16 SEAD capability proves to be inadequate.

The engine compartment looking towards the air intake. The engine normally fits flush to the hole in the center. Most of this structure is made of titanium, and the F-15 was one of the first fighters with a fire extinguishing system built into the engine compartment. The aircraft also has an armored bulkhead between the engines, made to protect the second engine in case of a catastrophic failure of one engine. (Todd Enlund)

RUFFLED FEATHERS

In 1983, McDonnell Douglas released a report that claimed the F-15 was credited with 54.5 confirmed kills, including: 23.5 MiG-21s, three MiG-23s, three MiG-25s, 24 MiGs of unspecified types, and a single helicopter. Another two MiG-21s were claimed as probably kills. Not mentioned in this report, but clearly evident to any interested observer, was that all of these kills were credited to the IDF/AF. This number has not been verified by independent sources, and most other observers are hard pressed to account for more than 35-40 confirmed kills.

By late 1978, the IDF/AF had received its original order for 25 F-15A/Bs, and the No. 133 squadron was considered operational with the type. By early 1979 the unit had scored its first 13 kills. The first IDF/AF action using F-15s took place on 27 June 1979 when a mixed force of F-15s and IAI Kfirs provided top cover for other IDF/AF aircraft carrying out an attack on terrorist bases near Sidon in southern Lebanon. A number of Syrian MiG-21s attempted to intercept the attacking force, but Israeli Grumman E-2 Hawkeye AWACS aircraft directed the top cover against them. The F-15s launched AIM-7s against a group of Syrian MiG-21s, but the Sparrows proved to be ineffective and in the dogfight that followed the F-15s killed four MiG-21s, while a Kfir C2 claimed a fifth, all with Sidewinder or Shafrir short-range missiles.

Another seven Syrian MiG-21s were shot down over Lebanon by December 1980, including four on 24 September 1979, one on 24 August 1980, and two on 31 December 1980. The F-15's next confirmed kill was of more significance since it was the first ever of a MiG-25. On 13 February 1981, a pair of IDF/AF RF-4Es penetrated Lebanon at 40,000 feet flying at more than Mach 1. Two Syrian MiG-25s were scrambled to intercept, and a few minutes later the RF-4Es released chaff and turned away from the Foxbats. A single F-15 had been flying below the RF-4s, and in a planned maneuver, zoom-climbed to 30,000 feet and fired an AIM-7F against a MiG-25 that was 10,000 feet above and moving towards the F-15. The MiG was destroyed, and the other MiG-25 broke off the engagement. A second MiG-25 was shot down by a F-15 on 29 July 1981.

The war in Lebanon in June 1982 brought a reported 36.5 additional victories for the IDF/AF F-15s. These included a pair of MiG-23MFs on 25

Israeli F-15C #840, named Commando (in Hebrew on the radome), shows six kill marks on the forward fuselage. Other than the adapters, barely visible on the wing pylons, for Python air-to-air missiles, the aircraft is mostly similar to its USAF counterparts. Most Israeli F-15s are named, with single-seat aircraft using one word names, while two-seaters use two-word names. (Tsahi Ben-Ami)

June, and a MiG-25 downed over Beirut on 31 August after it was first damaged by a MIM-23B Improved Hawk SAM (hence, only a half kill for the F-15). None of the F-15s were lost during this conflict, although one was severely damaged on 9 June by a surface to air missile, but its pilot managed to limp it to a landing at Ramat-David AB, demonstrating the excellent behavior of the F-15 after suffering battle damage, or any other type of damage for that matter.

The ultimate demonstration of the F-15's ability to survive an amazing amount of damage came on 1 May 1983 when an F-15D (#957, nicknamed "Markia Shchakim") collided with an A-4N Skyhawk during an air combat training mission. The Skyhawk's pilot ejected, but the F-15's crew, failing to realize they had lost their entire right wing, managed to land the damaged F-15 at a nearby air base. The aircraft touched down at 260 knots, roughly twice the normal landing speed. The F-15 was repaired and returned to service two months later.

At least five IDF/AF F-15s have been lost in accidents. An F-15A was lost in August 1981 after flying through a flock of storks, and the second was lost on 2 April 1987 when an F-15C inadvertently went into a spin during an air combat training mission. The pilot waited until the last minute to attempt to eject, but his ejection seat malfunctioned, killing the pilot. On 15 August 1988, two F-15As collided during an air combat training mission. The Israelis have since modified their air combat instrumentation system to include a warning of collision courses on the pilot's HUD. A F-15D was lost in January, 1997.

Kill markings adorn F-15C 85-0114 from the 58th TFS. Somewhat confusingly, the aircraft, like several others from the Gulf War, wears two sets of kills. The single dark green star by Capt. Tony Schiavi's name indicates that he scored a victory against a MiG 23 on 26 January 1991, except he was flying 85-0108 at the time. The two Iraqi flags mark victories by Capt. Caesar Rodriguez on 19 January (a MiG 29) and 26 January (a MiG 23) while he was flying this aircraft. The aircraft carries all the latest 1996 upgrades, including the modified windscreen and the forward ALQ-135 antennas above and below the nose. (Mick Roth Collection)

During the Gulf War, IDF/AF F-15s were maintained at a high degree of readiness, including around-the-clock combat air patrols from August 1990 until February 1991. Although the Israeli F-15s were not directly involved in the Gulf War, they indirectly benefited from the conflict. Since 1986, when the advanced MiG-29 entered service in Syria, the Israelis had a sense of uncertainty about the outcome of an air combat between the F-15 and the MiG-29. The USAF F-15 kills

The F-15C/Ds began to fly combat air patrols in cooperation with Saudi F-15Cs and British and Saudi Tornado F.Mk 3s, whereas the F-15Es began to train for the strike mission should that become necessary. During such a training mission, an F-15E (87-0203) crashed on 30 September 1990, killing both crewmen.

Capt. Steve Tate from the 71st TFS used this F-15C (83-0017) to shoot down an Iraqi Mirage F.1EQ on 17 January 1991 with an AIM-7. A single green star under the pilot's name proclaims this kill. (Mick Roth Collection)

A second round of Desert Shield buildups took place in November 1990 when the F-15C-equipped 58th TFS, deployed to Tabuk in western Saudi Arabia. The 53rd TFS also deployed to Tabuk. Aircraft of the 7440th Composite Wing joined the 525th TFS and 32nd TFS based at Incirlik in Turkey. A second F-15E squadron, the 335th TFS from Seymour Johnson, moved to Al Kharj.

of several MiG-29s during Desert Storm eased these concerns considerably, and led directly to the 1994 order for 25 F-15Is.

AMERICAN AND SAUDI EAGLES JOIN THE FRAY

On 1 August 1990, Iraqi forces invaded Kuwait and five days later a multi-national coalition led by the United States launched Operation Desert Shield to defend against any Iraqi moves southward against

Saudi Arabia. The 1st TFW at Langley AFB deployed its F-15C/Ds to Dhahran in Saudi Arabia and on 12 August F-15Es from the 336th TFS at Seymour Johnson AFB left for the Gulf.

During Operations Desert Shield and Desert Storm, 120 F-15C/Ds deployed to the Persian Gulf and flew more than 5,900 sorties. Forty-eight F-15Es were deployed to the Gulf and flew more than 2,200 sorties.

Desert Storm began on the morning of 17 January 1991, and 37 enemy aircraft were destroyed by USAF F-15s during the Gulf War, mostly by pilots of the 58th TFS, against zero losses. Every Iraqi fixed-wing aircraft destroyed in air-to-air combat, including five Soviet-made MiG-29 Fulcrums, were downed by F-15s. No coalition air-

This F-15D (79-0010) is easily identifiable as one of the F-15s hurriedly transferred from USAF stocks to the Royal Saudi Air Force at the beginning of the Gulf War. The ALQ-128 antenna on the left vertical stabilizer was not included on any foreign aircraft except the 24 ex-USAF Eagles transferred in August 1990. These markings are typical of those found on all Saudi F-15C/Ds, with "Royal Saudi Air Force" written in Arabic and English on the nose, and a Saudi flag on the vertical stabilizer. Other than not having some of the more sensitive ECM equipment, Saudi aircraft are identical to USAF F-15s. (Department of Defense)

craft were lost to Iraqi fighters. Most of the kills were made at long range by the AIM-7 Sparrow, which had performed so poorly in Vietnam but which turned in an outstanding performance in the Gulf War. Nine kills were made by the F-15C with AIM-9 Sidewinders, and one kill was credited to a F-15C pilot who maneuvered his opponent into flying his MiG-29 into the ground. The single kill by an F-15E, against an unidentified helicopter, used a laser-guided bomb. The F-15's 20MM cannon was never fired in anger during Desert Storm, nor was the AIM-120 missile, although there were more than 1,000 "captive carries" of the AIM-120A during combat missions in the last few days of the war.

During Desert Shield/Storm, RSAF F-15s flew combat air patrols along with their American counterparts, and on 24 January 1991, Captain Ayehid Salah al-Shamrani of the No. 13 Squadron shot down a pair of Iraqi Mirage F1s that were flying along the Persian Gulf coast.

No F-15C/D Eagles were lost in combat, although two F-15Es were shot down by ground fire, one on 18 January (88-1689) and one (88-1692) the next day. The crew of the first plane were killed, the crew of the second were taken prisoner, but subsequently released.

After the war was officially over F-15Cs continued to carry out patrols to enforce the "no-fly" zone imposed under the terms of the cease-fire. On 22 March 1991, an F-15C (84-0014) shot down an Iraqi Su-22 with an AIM-9. On 24 March, an F-15C (84-0010) from the 53rd TFS shot down another Su-22 violating the no-fly order. Another F-15C was able to claim a Pilatus

The 33rd TFW's commanding officer's aircraft (85-0102) is named "Gulf Spirit" and sports a stylized Florida logo on both sides of the forward fuselage. The left side still proves more interesting, however, since the Iraqi kill marks only appear on that side. (David F. Brown via the Mick Roth Collection)

PC-9 trainer which was flying in close vicinity of the downed Su-22 when its pilot bailed out without a shot being fired. In addition, a two-seat F-15E scored a kill by dropping a laser-guided bomb on an airborne Iraqi helicopter on 14 February.

On 14 April 1994, there was a tragic "friendly fire" incident over northern Iraq, when a pair of F-15Cs of the 52nd Fighter Wing enforcing the "no-fly" rule mistakenly shot down two UH-60 Blackhawk helicopters, killing 26 American and United Nations personnel who were carrying out humanitarian aid to Kurdish areas of Iraq. One of the helicopters was destroyed by an AIM-120, the other by an AIM-9.

In September 1996, USAF F-15s again found themselves on the way to Saudi Arabia in response to renewed aggression by Iraq against the Kurds. During a heated exchange of words, several surface to air missiles were launched against US aircraft patrolling the "no-fly" zone, but none were damaged. The F-15s returned home in early 1997 without firing a shot.

Col. Rick Parsons, the current commander, scored a single Su-22 kill while flying 85-0124 on 7 February 1991, and this is confirmed by the single green star next to his name. 85-0102 was used by Capt. David Rose on 29 January against a MiG 23, while Capt. Murphy used the aircraft to kill two Su-22s on 7 February 1991. (Kenneth Kula via the Mick Roth Collection)

Armament

Fixed armament for all variants of the F-15 consists of a single General Electric M61A1 20MM Vulcan rotary cannon in the shoulder area of the right wing root. The muzzle is positioned well aft of the engine air intake to prevent ingestion of exhaust gases. The cannon has six barrels, weighs 275 pounds, is electrically controlled, hydraulically driven, and has a muzzle velocity of 3,380 feet per second. The gun has a selectable firing rate of 4,000 or 6,000 rounds per minute, and a total of 940 rounds of ammunition are carried by all variants except the F-15E. A drum assembly provides storage for the 20MM ammunition, and is directly linked to the ammunition conveyer system and the return conveyer system. An exit unit removes ammunition from the drum and an entrance unit returns spent cases, misfired rounds and cleared rounds to the drum. The complete ammunition cycle forms a closed loop from the ammunition drum to the gun and return.

In order to gain additional space for electronic equipment (primarily the ALQ-135 set), the F-15E variants have a redesigned ammunition handling system that uses a linkless feed system. The ammunition capacity was initially stated as 512 rounds, but ever increasing need for volume for the electronics has reduced this to 450 rounds in current production aircraft. The new system required the use of a small fairing on the underside of the fuselage directly beneath the

A fairly typical war-load of missiles—AIM-120s on the fuselage stations and inboard pylon, with an AIM-9 on the outboard pylon. Unlike the 1970s, when missiles were generally painted gloss white, modern missiles are a dull light gray to help them blend into the aircraft's camouflage. Due to the F-15's poor fuel fraction, a centerline tank is almost always present when conformal fuel tanks are not carried. (Dennis R. Jenkins)

AIM-120s on the fuselage stations and inboard pylon, with an AIM-9 on the outboard pylon is becoming the normal combat load. This is the pylon configuration preferred by pilots since mounting the AIM-9 on the inboard position blocks part of its seeker view, making lock-on harder to achieve while maneuvering. However, the ground crews do not like loading the AIM-120 on the inboard position due to its weight and limited access between the mounting rail and the fuselage. (Dennis R. Jenkins)

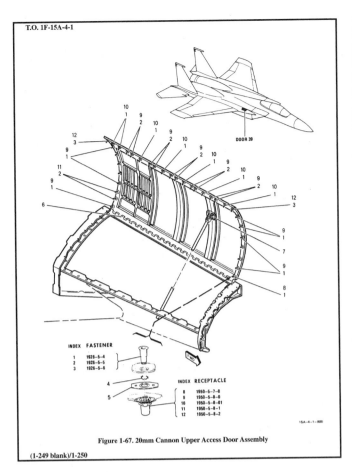

M61A1 GUN SYSTEM

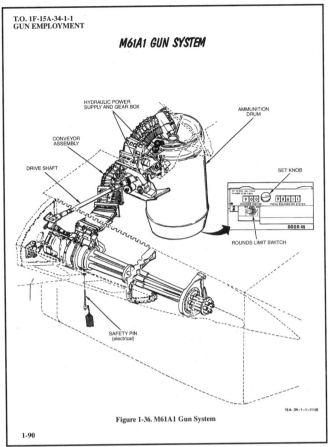

INDEX	FASTENER
1	1926-5-4
2	1926-5-5
3	1926-5-6

INDEX	RECEPTACLE
8	1950-5-7-0
9	1950-5-8-0
10	1950-5-8-01
11	1950-5-8-1
12	1950-5-8-2

15A-4-1-(68)

Figure 1-67. 20mm Cannon Upper Access Door Assembly

(1-249 blank)/1-250

1-90

15A-34-1-1-(11)E

Figure 1-36. M61A1 Gun System

The F-15 uses the same General Electric M61A1 Vulcan 20mm rotary cannon that has been used on almost every US fighter for the past thirty years. Originally a new 25mm cannon that fired caseless ammunition was scheduled to be installed in the F-15. However, difficulties developing the ammunition for the GAU-7A led to its being cancelled prior to the F-15's first flight. During the F-X development phase, there was even talk of developing directed-energy weapons (lasers) that could equip the F-15 later in its career. The airborne lasers have finally arrived, but they require a Boeing 747 to carry them! Noteworthy in these illustrations from the F-15 weapons manuals is how the ammunition drum changed shape between the air-superiority F-15s (top right) and the F-15E (bottom right). (U.S. Air Force)

M61A1 GUN SYSTEM

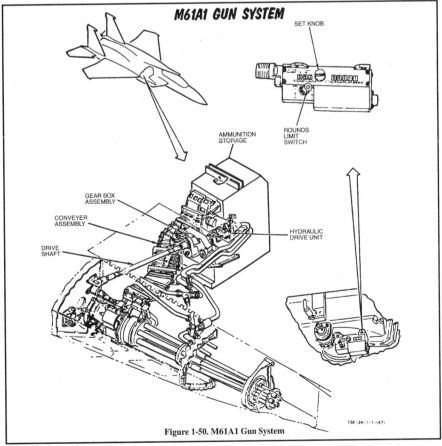

15E-34-1-1-(47)

Figure 1-50. M61A1 Gun System

The aft fuselage station initially proved to be hostile to the AIM-120, causing premature failure due to vibration loads. Subsequent modification to the missile allowed it to be carried without fear of failure. The small "wing" above the AIM-120 was installed to assist the AIM-7 to separate from the fuselage cleanly. Early F-15As were not equipped with this flow separator. (Dennis R. Jenkins)

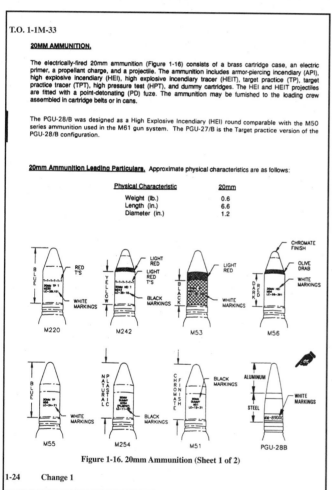

T.O. 1-1M-33

20MM AMMUNITION.

The electrically-fired 20mm ammunition (Figure 1-16) consists of a brass cartridge case, an electric primer, a propellant charge, and a projectile. The ammunition includes armor-piercing incendiary (API), high explosive incendiary (HEI), high explosive incendiary tracer (HEIT), target practice (TP), target practice tracer (TPT), high pressure test (HPT), and dummy cartridges. The HEI and HEIT projectiles are fitted with a point-detonating (PD) fuze. The ammunition may be furnished to the loading crew assembled in cartridge belts or in cans.

The PGU-28/B was designed as a High Explosive Incendiary (HEI) round comparable with the M50 series ammunition used in the M61 gun system. The PGU-27/B is the Target practice version of the PGU-28/B configuration.

20mm Ammunition Leading Particulars. Approximate physical characteristics are as follows:

Physical Characteristic	20mm
Weight (lb.)	0.6
Length (in.)	6.6
Diameter (in.)	1.2

Figure 1-16. 20mm Ammunition (Sheet 1 of 2)

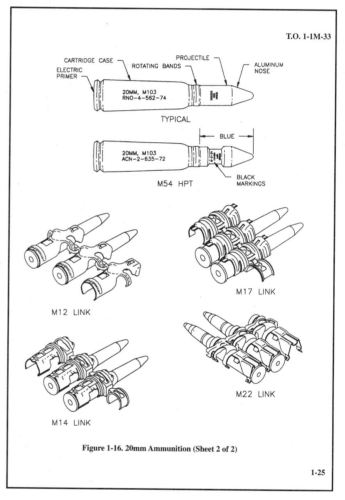

T.O. 1-1M-33

Figure 1-16. 20mm Ammunition (Sheet 2 of 2)

The components that make up a complete round or cartridge used in the M61A1 cannon are: a brass or steel cartridge case, an electric primer, propellant powder, and the projectile. The complete cartridge is approximately 6.625 inches long and weighs roughly 1/2 pound. Three types of ammunition are currently available. The 20MM target practice cartridge (TP) is ball ammunition with a hollow projectile that does not contain filler. The 20MM armor piercing incendiary (API) projectile is charged with an incendiary composition that ignites on impact. And the 20MM high explosive incendiary (HEI) cartridge explodes with an incendiary effect after it has penetrated the target. The HEI cartridge is normally used against aircraft and light ground targets. (U.S. Air Force)

ammunition drum, and this is one of the identifying features of the Strike Eagle.

The basic F-15 is equipped with nine external stores stations: the left outboard wing station is #1; the left inboard wing station is #2, the left forward fuselage missile station is #3 while the left aft fuselage missile station is #4; the centerline is #5; the right fuselage missile stations are #6 (forward) and #7 (aft); the right inboard wing station is #8; and the right outboard wing station is #9. The inboard wing station pylons are both equipped with two rail launchers for AIM-9/AIM-120 missiles, effectively giving four additional stations. Stations #1 and #9 were intended for a still-born ECM pod, and are not

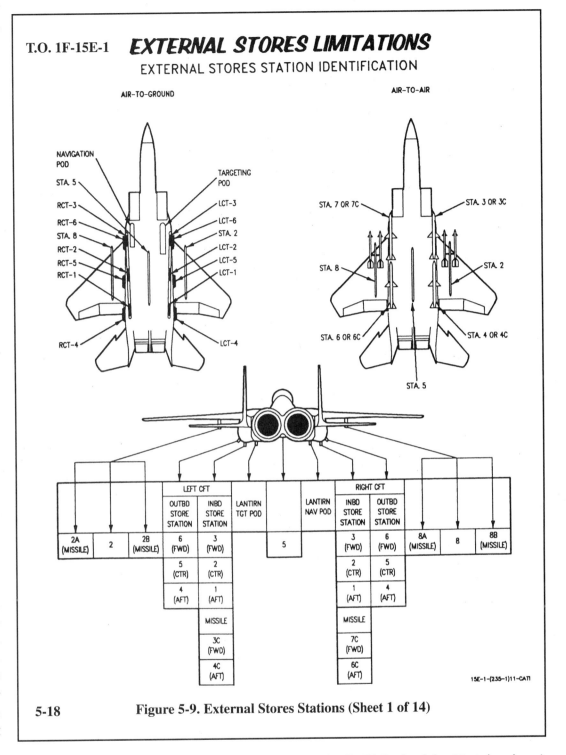

T.O. 1F-15E-1 ***EXTERNAL STORES LIMITATIONS***
EXTERNAL STORES STATION IDENTIFICATION

5-18   **Figure 5-9. External Stores Stations (Sheet 1 of 14)**

15E-1-(235-1)11-CAT1

The type-4 conformal fuel tanks added eight additional stores stations to the F-15E. Each of the 12 stub pylons is capable of carrying up to 2,000 pounds of air-to-ground weapons, and four of them are wired to support the same AIM-7 and AIM-120 air-to-air missiles normally carried by the F-15 on the corners of the air intakes. It is unusual to see anything on the centerline station other than a 610 gallon fuel tank, but it is wired to support a multitude of air-to-ground weapons. During the Gulf War, the F-15E carried special "bunker buster" 4,000 pound bombs that had been hastily constructed using surplus 8-inch naval cannon barrels. One of these weapons could be carried under each wing. The F-15E and its variants finally deleted the outer wing hardpoints which had been designed for a still-born ECM pod, but had never been cleared to carry any weapons, although AGM-88 HARMs have been observed there on occasion. (U.S. Air Force)

McDonnell Douglas
F-15 EAGLE

87

The forward fuselage station with an AIM-120 missile. The use of the fuselage corners to carry missiles allows the three main hard points (one under each wing and the centerline fuselage) to be used for fuel or other weapons without compromising the aircraft's ability to fight. Most early artist concepts of the F-15 showed two of the proposed AIM-82 short-range dog-fight missiles on this station, but as built, only a single AIM-7 or AIM-120 can be carried here. Carriage of the AIM-120 involved modifying the "eagle claw" attachment fitting to accommodate the new missile. (Dennis R. Jenkins)

currently cleared to carry any stores. The outboard wing stations (#1 and #9) were finally deleted from the F-15E/I/S variants.

The F-15 is capable of carrying a variety of air-to-air missiles including the AIM-7F/M Sparrow III, AIM-9L/M/P Sidewinder,

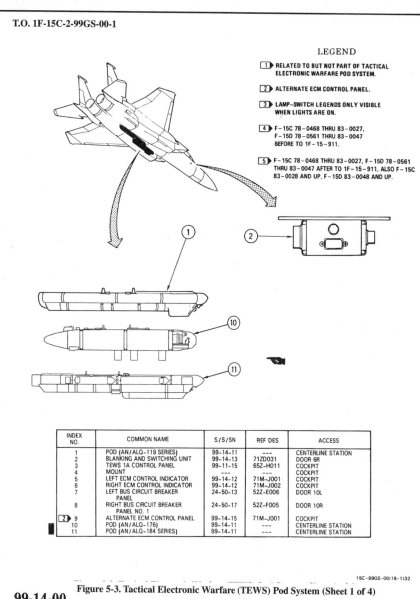

T.O. 1F-15C-2-99GS-00-1

LEGEND

1 ▶ RELATED TO BUT NOT PART OF TACTICAL ELECTRONIC WARFARE POD SYSTEM.

2 ▶ ALTERNATE ECM CONTROL PANEL.

3 ▶ LAMP-SWITCH LEGENDS ONLY VISIBLE WHEN LIGHTS ARE ON.

4 ▶ F-15C 78-0468 THRU 83-0027, F-15D 78-0561 THRU 83-0047 BEFORE TO 1F-15-911.

5 ▶ F-15C 78-0468 THRU 83-0027, F-15D 78-0561 THRU 83-0047 AFTER TO 1F-15-911, ALSO F-15C 83-0028 AND UP, F-15D 83-0048 AND UP.

INDEX NO.	COMMON NAME	S/S/SN	REF DES	ACCESS
1	POD (AN/ALQ-119 SERIES)	99-14-11	---	CENTERLINE STATION
2	BLANKING AND SWITCHING UNIT	99-14-13	71ZD031	DOOR 6R
3	TEWS 1A CONTROL PANEL	99-11-15	65Z-H011	COCKPIT
4	MOUNT	---	---	COCKPIT
5	LEFT ECM CONTROL INDICATOR	99-14-12	71M-J001	COCKPIT
6	RIGHT ECM CONTROL INDICATOR	99-14-12	71M-J002	COCKPIT
7	LEFT BUS CIRCUIT BREAKER PANEL	24-50-13	52Z-E006	DOOR 10L
8	RIGHT BUS CIRCUIT BREAKER PANEL NO. 1	24-50-17	52Z-F005	DOOR 10R
2 ▶ 9	ALTERNATE ECM CONTROL PANEL	99-14-15	71M-J001	COCKPIT
10	POD (AN/ALQ-176)	99-14-11	---	CENTERLINE STATION
11	POD (AN/ALQ-184 SERIES)	99-14-11	---	CENTERLINE STATION

15C-99GS-00(18-1)32

Figure 5-3. Tactical Electronic Warfare (TEWS) Pod System (Sheet 1 of 4)

99-14-00

(5-16A blank)/5-16B   Change 28

All F-15s are capable of carrying an ECM pod on the centerline station, although this should be unnecessary on single-seat aircraft fitted with all the internal ECM systems. Two seat aircraft (except the F-15E variants) lack the internal ALQ-135 system, and need to carry a pod if they enter a high threat area. Three different pods have been cleared for carriage on the Eagle: ALQ-119 (top); ALQ-176; and ALQ-184 (bottom). Originally, the outboard weapons stations (#1 and #9) were designed to carry an unspecified still-born ECM pod. (U.S. Air Force)

WARBIRDTECH
S E R I E S

and the AIM-120A/B/C AMRAAM. The AIM-7s are carried on the four fuselage missile stations. The AIM-9s are rail launched, and are carried mounted on either side of each inboard wing station weapons pylon. AIM-120s may replace any of the AIM-7s and/or AIM-9s.

Each of the inboard wing stations and the centerline accommodate a variety of conventional and special stores carried singularly or on multiple ejector racks (MER). The MER-200 racks used on the F-15 are of a different design than earlier MERs, and are rated to 7.33g as opposed to the usual 5g.

The AIM-120 is unique, permitting either rail launch or drop-launching. This allows it to be mounted in place of either AIM-7 or AIM-9s as the situation dictates. The F-15 is capable of carrying eight AIM-120s. The AIM-120 is slightly smaller than the Sparrow, but significantly larger than the Sidewinder, although the new missile has a longer range than either. (Dennis R. Jenkins)

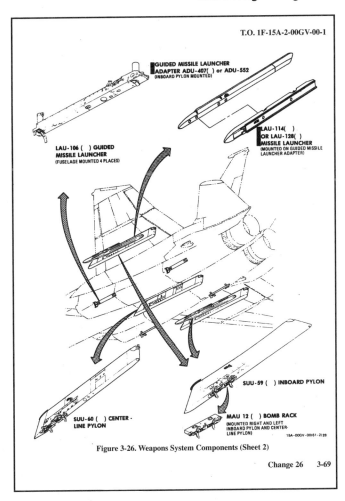

Figure 3-26. Weapons System Components (Sheet 2)

Change 26   3-69

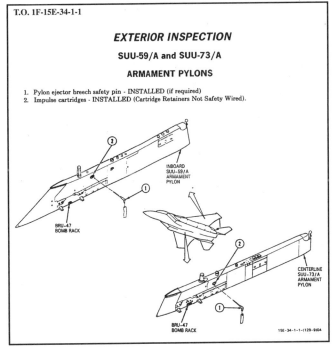

The two wing pylons are identical and interchangeable. Each wing pylon can be fitted with two launcher rails capable of carrying AIM-9 or AIM-120 missiles without interfering with the carriage of other stores on the main pylon. The LAU-106 guided missile adapter is normally fitted to the corners of the fuselage and used to mount AIM-7 or AIM-120 missiles. (U.S. Air Force)

The red flags attached to the missiles and other items are safing devices. Usually attached to pins, they permit ground crews to operate safely, and are large and visible enough to remind crews to remove them before flight. (Dennis R. Jenkins)

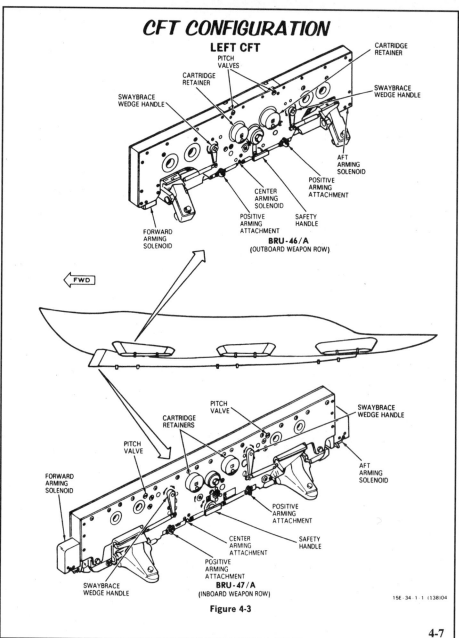

CFT CONFIGURATION

LEFT CFT

PITCH VALVES
CARTRIDGE RETAINER
CARTRIDGE RETAINER
SWAYBRACE WEDGE HANDLE
SWAYBRACE WEDGE HANDLE
AFT ARMING SOLENOID
POSITIVE ARMING ATTACHMENT
CENTER ARMING SOLENOID
POSITIVE ARMING ATTACHMENT
SAFETY HANDLE
FORWARD ARMING SOLENOID

BRU-46/A
(OUTBOARD WEAPON ROW)

FWD

PITCH VALVE
CARTRIDGE RETAINERS
PITCH VALVE
SWAYBRACE WEDGE HANDLE
AFT ARMING SOLENOID
FORWARD ARMING SOLENOID
POSITIVE ARMING ATTACHMENT
CENTER ARMING ATTACHMENT
SAFETY HANDLE
POSITIVE ARMING ATTACHMENT
SWAYBRACE WEDGE HANDLE

BRU-47/A
(INBOARD WEAPON ROW)

Figure 4-3

15E-34-1-1 (138)04

4-7

The type-4 conformal fuel tank (CFT) used on the F-15E (and its variants) contain up to six weapons stations each. Two of these stations can be used to carry AIM-7 or AIM-120 air-to-air missiles, but normally all six are used to carry air-to-ground ordnance. The low-drag CFTs contain approximately 114 cubic feet of usable volume and attach to the outer side of each engine intake, under the wing root. They are designed to the same load factors as the basic F-15 (i.e.; 9g) and can be installed or removed in 15 minutes. At subsonic and transonic speeds the CFTs actually improve the aircraft's drag coefficient (being slightly area-ruled), and impose a minimal penalty at supersonic speeds. The unit is designed for quick installation on the aircraft and is fitted to the fuselage of the F-15 using the standard USAF bomb lift truck with a simple adapter. Maintenance personnel raise it into position, install two bolts, and make one electrical and two fluid connections. The CFTs are not capable of being jettisoned, but the fuel can be dumped through the aircraft's normal dump system. (U.S. Air Force)

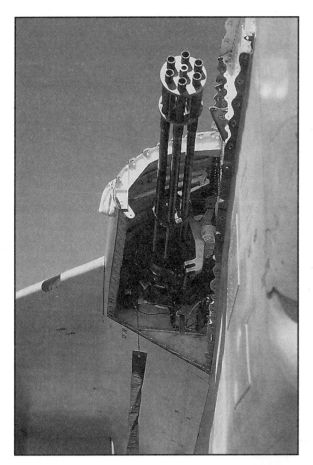

The General Electric M61A1 20mm Vulcan cannon is housed in the right wing root, while the ammunition drum is on the aircraft centerline, buried in the fuselage. The Vulcan is a six-barrel rotary cannon capable of firing at 6,000 rounds per minute. Unfortunately, the F-15 carries only 940 rounds (450 for the F-15E), limiting it to less than 10 seconds of shooting. And although the 20mm cannon is an effective weapon, the more modern 25mm and 30mm cannon used by the Russian and other air forces pack a greater punch. (Mick Roth)

Drop tanks containing 610 gallons may be carried on the three inboard stations of all F-15s. The tanks are rated to the same 9g limit as the basic airframe. The outboard wing stations, rated at 1,300 pounds each, are not currently cleared to carry any stores (according to the flight manual), although both ECM pods and HARM have been observed there on occasion.

All F-15s can carry and deliver laser-guided bombs such as the GBU-10E/B or GBU-12D/B Paveway II. However, only the F-15E variants have the capability of guiding these weapons, and earlier models must rely on laser designators carried by other aircraft or by personnel on the ground.

Among the weapons approved for the F-15A/B/C/D are: Mk 20 Rockeye, Mk 82, Mk 84, BLU-27,

The cannon is not visible at all when the skin panels are in place. The location of the cannon was largely dictated by a desire to mount it far enough back so that smoke would not enter the engine air intakes, a lesson-learned from the F-4E and other aircraft that had used nose-mounted cannon. The original plan for the F-15 were to use a new 25mm cannon that fired caseless ammunition. Unfortunately the new cannon ran into development and funding problems, and was cancelled prior to the F-15's first flight. (Dennis R. Jenkins)

Cooling air for the cannon is provided by a small grille just aft of the muzzle, while smoke is exhausted by the larger vent further aft. This area can become quite dirty after the cannon is fired. The vents on top of the air intake are part of the bleed air system. (Don Logan)

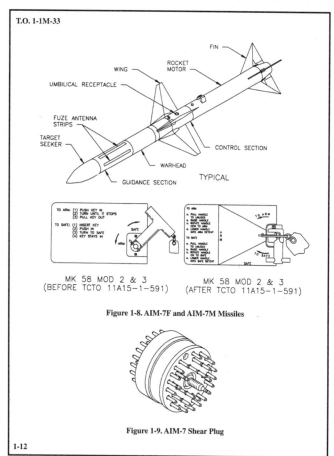

T.O. 1-1M-33

Figure 1-8. AIM-7F and AIM-7M Missiles

Figure 1-9. AIM-7 Shear Plug

1-12

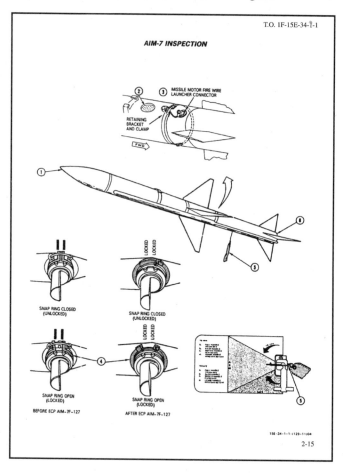

T.O. 1F-15E-34-1-1

AIM-7 INSPECTION

2-15

All variants of the F-15 are capable of carrying a variety of air-to-air missiles including the AIM-7F/M Sparrow III. The AIM-7 is a semi-active radar guided missile, but the target must be illuminated by the launching aircraft's radar for the entire flight. Up to four AIM-7s can be mounted on the corners of the air intake trunks, or on the corners of all types of conformal fuel tanks. The Sparrow's performance in the Gulf war was considered excellent. The AIM-7 is finally being replaced in the active inventory by the AIM-120 AMRAAM, although the sheer number of Sparrows that were purchased ensure it will be around for years to come. (U.S. Air Force)

WARBIRD**TECH**
SERIES

CBU-52, CBU-58, and CBU-71 bombs; the Matra Durandal runway denial weapon; SUU-20 training weapons; ALQ-119, ALQ-131, ALQ-176, and ALQ-184 ECM pods; and B61 nuclear stores (USAF aircraft only).

A partial listing of the F-15E/I/S's cleared stores includes: Mk 20 Rockeye, Mk 82, Mk 84, BDU-38, BLU-107, BSU-49, BSU-50, GBU-8, GBU-10, GBU-12, GBU-15, GBU-24, CBU-52, CBU-58, CBU-71, CBU-87, CBU-89, CBU-90, CBU-92, CBU-93 bombs; LAU-3A

Until the introduction of the AIM-120 AMRAAM, the F-15's primary medium-range missile was the AIM-7 Sparrow III. This missile had performed very poorly in Vietnam, but redeemed itself in Operation Desert Storm where it scored an impressive kill ratio. In the mid-1990s it finally began to be replaced by the AIM-120. (Dennis R. Jenkins)

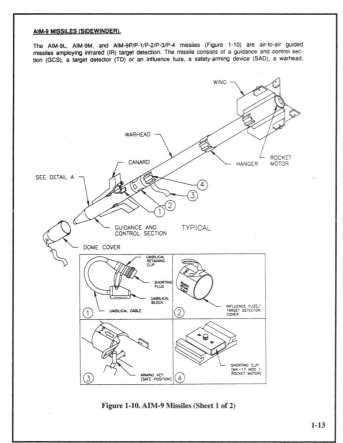

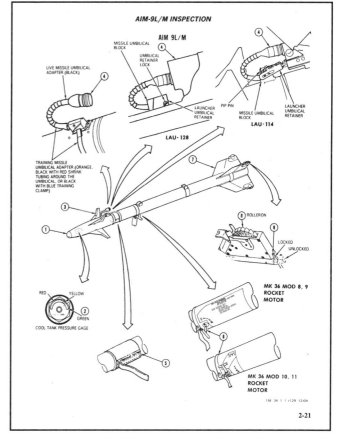

Three separate versions of the Sidewinder missile can be carried (AIM-9L/P/M). The Sidewinder is an infrared guided missile that homes in the heat generated by its target. The AIM-9s are rail launched, and are carried mounted on either side of each inboard wing station weapons pylon. AIM-120s may replace any of the AIM-9s. Ground crews do not like to mount the AIM-120 on the inboard wing rail because of handling problems, although flight crews do not like AIM-9s mounted on the inboard rails since it restricts the seeker's field of view. (U.S. Air Force)

rockets; SUU-20 training weapons; U-33 tow target; AGM-65 Mavericks; AGM-130; and B61 nuclear stores. An AXQ-14 data link pod is used in conjunction with the GBU-15 precision guided weapon, and is carried on the centerline station. LANTIRN navigation (AAQ-13) and targeting (AAQ-14) pods are carried on additional stations just aft of the lower edge of the air intakes.

All F-15 variants except the A/B are capable of carrying conformal fuel tanks (CFT), and these provide additional weapons stations. They attach to outer side of each engine intake, under the wing root, and are designed to the same load factors as the basic F-15 (i.e.; 9g). The CFTs can be installed or removed in 15 minutes. At subsonic and transonic speeds the CFTs actually improve the aircraft's drag coefficient (being slightly area-ruled), and impose a minimal penalty at supersonic speeds. All external stores stations remain available with the CFTs in place, and McDonnell Douglas has developed a new weapons attachment system which can extend the operating radius with large external loads by up to 40 percent. Known as tangential carriage, it involves the installation of six stations in two rows of stub pylons on the lower corner and bottom of each type-4 CFT. Each of these sta-

tions is capable of carrying 2,000 pounds, and four of them are wired to support AIM-7 or AIM-120 missiles. The use of tangential carriage greatly reduces the drag associated with carrying external stores when compared to the normal MERs. Early type-1 CFTs have attach points for four Sparrows, and are used primarily on F-15C/Ds instead of the F-15E.

The ASQ-T11 and ASQ-T13 air combat maneuvering instrumentation system pods may also be carried by all F-15 variants. The pod is the airborne portion of an ACMI training system, and contains a data link system that enables the

Unlike the type-4 CFTs carried by the F-15E, the type-1 CFTs carried by the F-15C/D are not equipped for tangential carriage. An effort to increase the weapons capacity of the F-15C/D involved the development of the type-3 CFT shown here that could accommodate a single MER, or the normal two AIM-7 Sparrows. Since the Air Force was not ready to commit the F-15C/D to the air-to-ground role, this type of CFT was not procured in any great numbers. Here the prototype units are shown on the first F-15C (78-0468) at Edwards. (Dennis R. Jenkins)

ground to monitor the aircraft's fire control system and flight instrumentation during air combat maneuvering training. The pod is the same general size and shape as a Sidewinder, and is suspended in the same manner as the AIM-9.

MXU-648/A cargo (personnel) pods may be carried on the inboard wing pylons and/or the centerline station. The pods are converted BLU-27 fire bomb shells and weigh 125 pounds. A maximum of 300 pounds may be loaded into each pod.

One of the few photographs showing the F-15 carrying weapons (an AGM-88 HARM) on the outboard wing station. This the Dual-Role Fighter evaluation aircraft (71-0291) just prior to it becoming the Strike Eagle demonstrator. The type-3 CFTs each carry a multiple ejector rack (MER) with six 500-pound bombs, along with a MER under each wing station and the centerline with more 500-pounders. Two AIM-9L Sidewinders on the inboard wing stations provide air-to-air capability. (McDonnell Douglas)

The new AIM-120 Advanced Medium-Range Air-to-Air Missile (AMRAAM) has been a long time in development, but finally began being used by operational units late in the Gulf War. Almost 1,000 flights were made with AIM-120s during Desert Storm, although none were fired in anger. The AMRAAM can replace any AIM-7 or AIM-9 on the F-15, and is capable of being either rail-launched (like the AIM-9) and drop-launched (like the AIM-7). The Eagle's normal combat load in 1996 has developed to be 2 AIM-7M on stations 3/7 (forward), 2 AIM-9s on stations 2B/8A (inboard), and 4 AIM-120s on stations 4/8 and 2A/8B. (U.S. Air Force)

AIM-120 MISSILE (AMRAAM).

The AIM-120A advanced medium-range air-to-air missile (AMRAAM) (Figure 1-11) is a supersonic homing missile equipped with active radar target detection and on-board inertial navigation guidance. The missile consists of guidance, warhead, propulsion, and control sections. The guidance section provides midcourse guidance and control, target acquisition, terminal guidance and control, and target encounter timing for warhead detonation. The warhead section contains a blast fragmentation warhead and a safing, arming, and fuzing (SAF) device that detonates the warhead. The SAF device prevents detonation of the warhead until a safe separation distance from the aircraft has been reached. The propulsion section contains the rocket motor, rocket motor arm/fire device (AFD), hooks for both rail and ejection launchers, flush-mounted umbilical, and the sockets for the four detachable wings. A buffer connector, supplied with each missile, provides connection between the flush-mounted missile umbilical and the launcher umbilical. An indicator visually shows the position of the AFD. "SAFE" is indicated by a white "S" on a green background, and "ARM" is indicated by a black "A" on a red background. The control section contains the complete control actuation system including the electronics and four fins. The missile is loaded and launched from a rail or ejection launcher.

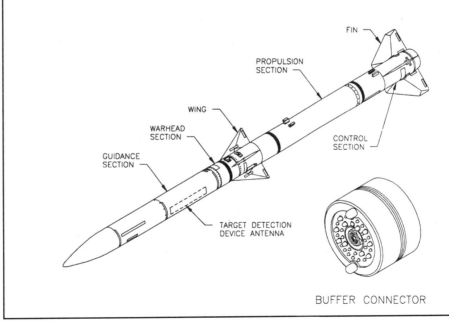

BLU-109 BOMB

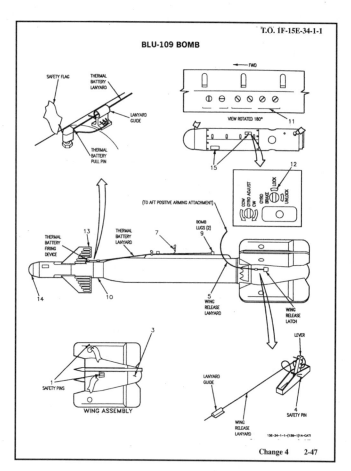

SAFETY FLAG
THERMAL BATTERY LANYARD
LANYARD GUIDE
THERMAL BATTERY PULL PIN

← FWD

VIEW ROTATED 180°

11

15

12

CCW GYRO ADJUST / CW GYRO BRAKE / LOCK UNLOCK

(TO AFT POSITIVE ARMING ATTACHMENT)

THERMAL BATTERY FIRING DEVICE
THERMAL BATTERY LANYARD
BOMB LUGS (2)

13   7   9
8

14   10   5

WING RELEASE LANYARD
WING RELEASE LATCH

LEVER

LANYARD GUIDE
WING RELEASE LANYARD
SAFETY PIN

SAFETY PINS

WING ASSEMBLY

15E-34-1-1-(129-1)14-CAT1

Change 4   2-47

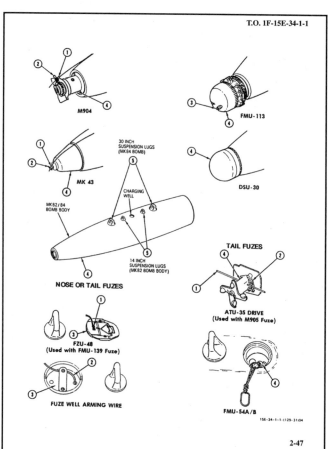

M904

FMU-113

MK 43

DSU-30

MK82/84 BOMB BODY

30 INCH SUSPENSION LUGS (MK84 BOMB)

CHARGING WELL

14 INCH SUSPENSION LUGS (MK82 BOMB BODY)

NOSE OR TAIL FUZES

TAIL FUZES

ATU-35 DRIVE (Used with M905 Fuze)

FZU-48 (Used with FMU-139 Fuze)

FUZE WELL ARMING WIRE

FMU-54A/B

15E-34-1-1-(129-31)04

2-47

GBU-15 INSPECTION

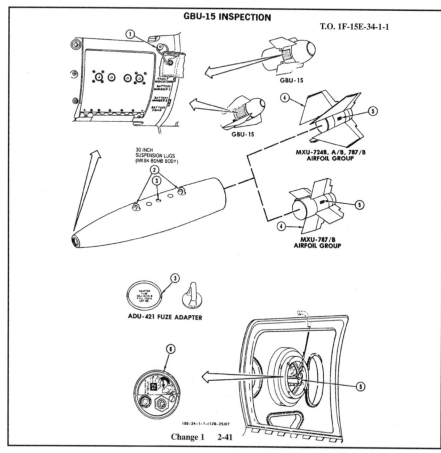

T.O. 1F-15E-34-1-1

GBU-15

GBU-15

MXU-724B, A/B, 787/B AIRFOIL GROUP

30 INCH SUSPENSION LUGS (MK84 BOMB BODY)

MXU-787/B AIRFOIL GROUP

ADU-421 FUZE ADAPTER

15E-34-1-1-(129-25)07

Change 1   2-41

The air-to-ground weapons cleared for carriage on the F-15E includes most all tactical bombs in the inventory. These include dumb iron bombs through precision TV and laser guided "smart" bombs. A partial listing of the F-15E's cleared stores includes: Mk 20 Rockeye, Mk 82, Mk 84, BLU-109, BSU-49, BSU-50, GBU-8, GBU-10, GBU-12, GBU-15, GBU-24, CBU-52, CBU-58, CBU-71, CBU-87, CBU-89, CBU-90, CBU-92, CBU-93 bombs; LAU-3A rockets; SUU-20 and SUU-30 training weapons; U-33 tow target; AGM-65 Mavericks; AGM-130; ALQ-119(V) ECM pods; and B61 nuclear stores. An AXQ-14 data link pod is used in conjunction with the GBU-15 precision guided weapon, and is carried on the centerline station. The maximum permissible external load for the F-15E/I/S is 36,000 pounds. (U.S. Air Force)

WARBIRDTECH
SERIES

EXTERIOR INSPECTION

GBU 24 BOMB

1. Switch settings - MATCH MISSION REQUIREMENT

2. Control module - CLEAN & UNDAMAGED

★3. Lanyard lock - SECURES LANYARD

★4. Fuze well arming wire - INSTALLED

5. Suspension lugs - ALIGNED & BASE OF LUG FLUSH WITH WEAPON SURFACE

6. Wing assembly fairing safety pins - REMOVED

7. Wing assembly safety pins - REMOVED

8. Tail fins - CLEAN & UNDAMAGED

★9. Release lever lanyard - INSTALLED & SAFETY PINS REMOVED.

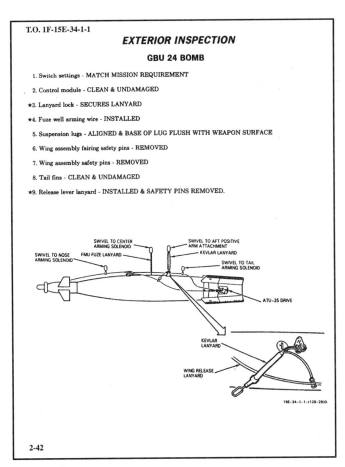

2-42

SUU-30 INSPECTION

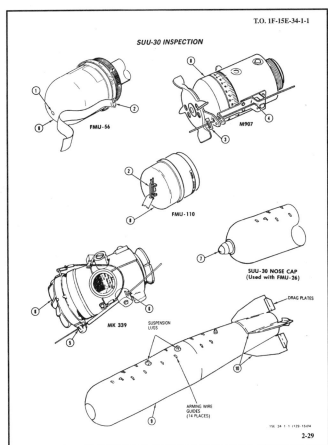

2-29

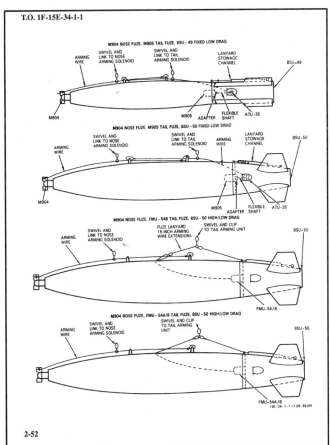

2-52

CBU-87 AND CBU-89 INSPECTION

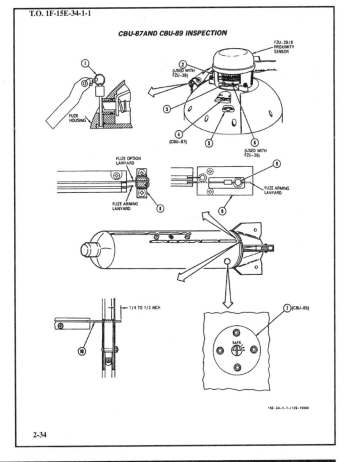

2-34

F-15 PROTOTYPES

SERIAL NUMBER	McAIR NUMBER	FIRST FLIGHT	FUNCTION
71-0280	F1	27 July, 1972	Envelope exploration, heandling qualities, external stores carriage tests. Used by Air Force Recruiting Service as display, to Lackland AFB museum.
71-0281	F2	26 September, 1992	F100 engine tests, to NASA, returned to USAF to Langley AFB museum.
71-0280	F3	4 November, 1972	Avioncis development, first AN/APG-63 equipped aircrat, calibrated airspeed tests.
71-0283	F4	13 January, 1973	Structural flight test aircraft.
71-0284	F5	7 March, 1973	Internal cannon testing, armament testing, stores jettison tests, first M61 equipped a/c, converted to ground systems trainer.
71-0285	F6	23 May, 1973	Avionics testing, flight control evaluation, missile firing evaluation, nicknamed "Killer."
71-0286	F7	14 June, 1973	Armament, fuel and stores testing, converted to ground systems trainer.
71-0290	T1	7 July, 1973	Two-seat evaluation, advanced concepts demonstrator, S/MTD test aircraft, F-15/ACTIVE
71-0287	F8	25 August, 1973	Spin tests, h igh AOA evaluation, to NASA as 835.
71-0291	T2	18 October, 1973	Bailed to McAir as demonstator, World tour, Strike Eagle prototype.
71-0289	F10	16 January, 1974	Radar and Avionics testbed.
72-0113	F11		Operational tests, conformal fuel tank tests, to RADC for electronic emmision tests.
72-0114	F12		Operational tests (first ECM-equipped a/c).
72-0115	F13		Operational tests.
72-0116	F14		Climatic (environmental) tests, nicknamed "Homer," to Israel in Peace Fox I.
72-0117	F15		Not used in AFDT&E, to Israel in Peace Fox I.
72-0118	F16		Operational tests/demonstrations, to Israel in Peace Fox I.
72-0119	F17		Project Streak Eagle, to Air Force Museum.
72-0120	F18		Not used in AFDT&E, to Israel in Peace Fox I.

SIGNIFICANT DATES

1951
USAF racks up outstanding 7:1 kill ratio against North Korean MiGs.

1962
John Boyd begins to study a theory on energy maneuverability.

1963
Project Forecast is released identifying future weapons requirements.

AUGUST 1964
Force Options for Tactical Air study initiated under Lt. Col. John W. Bohn, Jr.

MAY 1964
John Boyd and Thomas Christie release a two-volunne report on Energy Maneuverability.

1965
USAF racks up a rather dismal 2.5:1 kill ratio against North Vietnamese MiGs.

7 JANUARY, 1965
Secretary of Defense McNamara allocates $10,000,000 to study new fighters.

27 FEBRUARY, 1965
Force Options for Tactical Air study completed; critical of large, expensive fighters.

APRIL 1965
Lt. Gen. James Ferguson establishes a working group to study medium-cost fighters.

6 OCTOBER, 1965
QOR-65-14-F outlines the need for a new air-superiority fighter.

8 DECEMBER, 1965
RFP released for F-X initial parametric design studies.

OCTOBER 1966
Major John Boyd joins the Air Staff Directorate of Requirements.

MARCH 1967
The F-X Concept Formulation Package and Technical Development Plan are ready.

28 APRIL, 1967
McDonnell Aircraft Company and Douglas Aircraft Company merge to form McDonnell Douglas

JULY 1967
The Russians hold the Domodadovo air show and show the new MiG-25 for the first time.

11 AUGUST, 1967
A second round of F-X studies begin at an increased priority.

DECEMBER 1967
USAF and Navy agree to jointly develop the F100 turbofan engine.

FEBRUARY 1968
Required Operational Capability requirement ROC-9-68 is released, calling for the F-X.

8 APRIL, 1968
RFPs are released for the development of the F100 turbofan.

MAY 1968
The F-X is assigned as the Air Force's top priority development program.

AUGUST 1968
Hughes is awarded a contract to build the new APG-63 radar for the F-15.

12 SEPTEMBER, 1968
The Air Force requests a designation for F-X, receives F-15.

30 DECEMBER, 1968
F-X study contracts issued to Fairchild-Republic, McDonnell Douglas and North American.

30 JUNE, 1969
F-15 technical proposals are submitted.

AUGUST 1969
F-15 cost and schedule proposals are submitted.

23 DECEMBER, 1969
McDonnell Douglas is announced as the winner of the F-15 contract.

27 MARCH, 1970
Pratt & Whitney is selected to develop the F100 turbofan engine.

MARCH 1970
Contracts are awarded for the development of the XAIM-82A short-range dogfight missile for the F-15.

SEPTEMBER 1970
The XAIM-82 short-range dogfight missile is cancelled by the Air Force.

NOVEMBER 1970
The Navy pares its F100 engine request from 179 units to just 69.

SIGNIFICANT DATES

22 JUNE, 1971
The Navy pulls out of the F100 turbo-fan engine program.

21 DECEMBER, 1971
Philco-Ford is selected to develop a new GAU-7A 25MM cannon for the F-15.

FEBRUARY 1972
The F100 turbofan engine completes its preliminary flight rating test.

26 JUNE, 1972
The first F-15 (71-0280) is rolled out in St. Louis.

27 JULY, 1972
The first F-15 (71-0280) makes its first flight at Edwards AFB with Irv Burrows at the controls.

NOVEMBER 1972
The Air Force cancels the GAU-7A 25mm cannon project: the F-15 will use the M61 20mm cannon.

MAY 1973
The F100 turbofan engine completes its final qualification test under controversy.

12 OCTOBER, 1973
The F100 turbofan engine completes an unmodified final qualification test.

27 JULY, 1974
The FAST-Pack concept makes its first flight aboard TF-15A 72-0291.

14 NOVEMBER, 1974
First operational F-15 (73-0108) delivered to USAF for training.

JANUARY 1975
Project Streak Eagle shatters all existing time-to-climb records.

15 OCTOBER, 1975
The first F-15 is lost after a fleet-wide 7,300 flight hours.

9 JANUARY, 1976
First operational unit (1st TFW) receives its initial F-15s.

10 DECEMBER, 1976
The first Israeli F-15 (72-0116) land at Tel-Nof AB, Isreal.

OCTOBER 1978
All TF-15As are redesignated F-15Bs.

26 FEBRUARY, 1979
The first F-15C (78-0468) makes its first flight.

27 JUNE, 1979
The IDF/AF makes the F-15's first kill: a Syrian MiG-21.

4 JUNE, 1980
The first Japanese F-15J (79-0280) makes its first flight.

13 FEBRUARY, 1981
AN IDF/AF scores the first kill of a MiG-25 using an F-15.

11 AUGUST, 1981
The first Saudi Arabian F-15 lands in Saudi Arabia.

AUGUST 1981
The Strike Eagle demonstrator (71-0291) makes its first flight.

21 JANUARY, 1984
The first launch of the Vought ASM-135 ASAT missile by an F-15 occurs at Edwards AFB.

24 FEBRUARY, 1984
The F-15E is selected as the Air Force's interdiction aircraft.

5 JULY, 1984
The RSAF scores its first kill with the F-1: an Iranian F-4E.

13 SEPTEMBER, 1985
An F-15A (77-0084) shoots down a satellite (Solwind 78-1) in the only operational ASAT test.

11 DECEMBER, 1986
The first F-15E (86-0183) makes its first flight.

7 SEPTEMBER, 1988
The S/MTD demonstrator (71-0290) makes its first flight fully configured.

17 JANUARY, 1991
The USAF scores its first kill with the F-15: an Iraqi MiG-29.

19 JUNE, 1995
The first F-15S (93-0852) makes its first flight.

24 APRIL, 1996
The F-15 ACTIVE (71-0290) performs the first supersonic thrust vectoring.

31 OCTOBER, 1996
The F-15 ACTIVE (71-0290) performs the first Mach 2 thrust vectoring.